Helping You Talking Toddler

Unlocking the Secrets to Early Language Development and Overcoming Speech Delays

Alyssa Flemmings

© **Copyright 2023 - All rights reserved.**

The content contained within this book may not be reproduced, duplicated, or transmitted without direct written permission from the author or the publisher.
Under no circumstances will any blame or legal responsibility be held against the publisher, or author, for any damages, reparation, or monetary loss due to the information contained within this book. Either directly or indirectly.

Legal Notice:
This book is copyright protected. This book is only for personal use. You cannot amend, distribute, sell, use, quote, or paraphrase any part, or the content within this book, without the consent of the author or publisher.

Disclaimer Notice:
Please note the information contained within this document is for educational and entertainment purposes only. All effort has been executed to present accurate, up-to-date, and reliable, complete information. No warranties of any kind are declared or implied. Readers acknowledge that the author is not engaging in rendering legal, financial, medical or pro, or professional advice. The content within this book has been derived from various sources. Please consult a licensed professional before attempting any techniques outlined in this book.
By reading this document, the reader agrees that under no circumstances is the author responsible for any direct or indirect losses incurred as a result of the use of the information

contained within this document, including, but not limited to,
— errors, omissions, or inaccuracies.

Table of Contents

INTRODUCTION 6

CHAPTER 1.   UNDERSTANDING TODDLER SPEECH DEVELOPMENT 13
- THE STAGES OF SPEECH DEVELOPMENT 14
- FACTORS THAT INFLUENCE SPEECH DEVELOPMENT 20
- WHEN TO EXPECT YOUR TODDLER TO START TALKING 24

CHAPTER 2.   RECOGNIZING THE SIGNS OF SPEECH DELAYS 26
- COMMON SIGNS OF SPEECH DELAYS 27
- HOW TO DIFFERENTIATE BETWEEN TYPICAL DELAYS AND MORE SEVERE ISSUES 35
- WHEN TO SEEK PROFESSIONAL HELP 39

CHAPTER 3.   THE POWER OF COMMUNICATION: GOING BEYOND WORDS 42
- IMPORTANCE OF NON-VERBAL COMMUNICATION 43
- ENCOURAGING GESTURES AND SIGNS 48
- FOSTERING EMOTIONAL CONNECTIONS 51

CHAPTER 4.   SETTING THE STAGE FOR SPEECH 55
- CREATING A LANGUAGE-RICH ENVIRONMENT 56
- ENCOURAGING IMITATION AND REPETITION 61
- USING AGE-APPROPRIATE TOYS AND ACTIVITIES 67

CHAPTER 5.   SIX-WEEK PLAN FOR GETTING YOUR TODDLER TO START TALKING - OVERVIEW 71
- INTRODUCTION TO THE 6-WEEK PLAN 73
- WEEKLY GOALS AND EXPECTATIONS 79

CHAPTER 6.   WEEK 1- BUILDING VOCABULARY 86
- INTRODUCING NEW WORDS 87
- LABELING OBJECTS AND ACTIONS 92
- UTILIZING EVERYDAY ACTIVITIES 95

CHAPTER 7.   WEEK 2- ENCOURAGING INTERACTION 101
- ENGAGING IN CONVERSATION 102
- ASKING OPEN-ENDED QUESTIONS 111
- PRAISING EFFORTS 114

CHAPTER 8.   WEEK- 3 READING AND STORYTELLING 117
　The Importance of reading aloud 118
　Choosing age-appropriate books 123
　Tips for engaging storytelling..128

CHAPTER 9.   WEEK 4 - SINGING AND MUSIC 132
　The Role of Music in language development 134
　Singing nursery rhymes and songs 139
　Encouraging Movement and Dance 142

CHAPTER 10.   WEEK 5 - PLAYTIME AND LANGUAGE....................146
　Play-based language activities..148
　Pretend play scenarios..152
　Interactive games and activities...156

CHAPTER 11.   WEEK 6 - REINFORCING PROGRESS AND MOVING FORWARD   161
　Assessing progress..162
　Overcoming challenges...165
　Continuing support beyond the 6-week plan 167

CHAPTER 12.   TIPS FOR MAINTAINING PROGRESS AND ADDRESSING SETBACKS...170
　Encouraging ongoing language development 171
　Handling setbacks and plateaus...174
　Seeking additional support when needed 176

CONCLUSION 180

Introduction

As a parent, you want what is best for your child. It can be frustrating and upsetting when they do not answer or speak to you. You may feel your child is not like the other kids in the playground and wonder whether something is wrong with them. Sometimes we must overcome our worries to recognize that this might be a phase for them, and everything will change quickly.

This book is to help you understand why it may be taking them a while to talk and what you can do to encourage them. It might also help to know that they are not alone and that other children worldwide have the same problem.

Children develop at different speeds, are often different in their development, and have different personalities. Therefore, it can be challenging for parents to tell what normal behavior is when they see their child communicating. Often behaviors last only a few weeks or months before they change or disappear altogether. These changes happen naturally and should not appear simultaneously for every child.

Many things can interfere with a child's ability to talk. Sometimes just getting everything in order is enough to help them begin to speak. Other times, a child may need some extra attention from the parent. This can be in terms of assisting them to get their thoughts together or ensuring they are not unhappy because the toddler does not speak. Some children may even need extra attention for these reasons and more.

Other times, it can be due to an outside event that triggers something inside their brain that suddenly causes them to think differently or better understand language and communication.

Sometimes, children must be encouraged to talk to their parents. These parents can make it seem like the child cannot communicate and that no one else understands them. This is untrue, and parents must encourage their children to communicate. It can also help if you let the child know that everyone understands them and that you will help them learn how to talk soon.

There are many reasons why this may happen to your toddler – but rest assured, there are reasons why they will speak too. Toddlers have difficulty communicating because they need to form their sentences while still learning their vocabulary. They do not understand grammar nearly as much as adults and make mistakes when trying to string together words immediately.

This book will help you understand your child and what may affect their ability to speak. It will give you some insight into the behaviors you can expect from them, things to watch out for, and what it means if they begin to communicate. Understanding their side of the communication problems will ensure that your efforts will not be in vain.

Parents need to remember that children are not intentionally trying to prevent them from understanding them or from preventing them from getting what they want. They have difficulty communicating with everyone because they are busy thinking about how they want to say something, most simply.

It can be concerning for parents when their toddler is not yet talking, especially when they see other children of the same age or younger speaking fluently. However, it's important to remember that each child develops at their own pace, and there is a wide range of what is considered "normal" for language development.

It is important not to get too frustrated and to enjoy the milestones your child is reaching while taking the time to try and understand their needs. It would be best if you were looking out for many things besides their communication difficulties, such as small motor skills, allergies, dietary issues, and more.

Sometimes it may feel like you can do nothing about a language delay in your infant or toddler. That's true for most children who experience delays caused by environmental factors or genetic disorders. Your toddler may also be experiencing delayed development in other areas, such as play skills or bedtime organization. By understanding the reason for their delay, you can start setting up the conditions needed to help them overcome their problems with communication.

Helping your toddler to talk might not be the first thing on your mind. You may be more concerned with cooking dinner, ensuring a clean diaper, or getting them ready to go out in public. As you understand what is happening in their world and learn what you can do or change around the house and outside, it will become easier for you. Getting through the initial stages of communication difficulties takes time, patience, and understanding.

Many parents have learned from a parent or other adults in the community that their child is not talking yet. They have put up with this for months or even years and are now at a point where they feel trapped.

These parents know that their genuine concerns should be about what is best for their child, and it can be so disheartening to hear others advise them to give up on their child. These people try to make the parents feel like they have failed when they have not reached this stage yet of language development. It is also upsetting because these adults criticize the parent's parenting skills, causing them more stress than they can handle.

If you are one of these parents, reading this book may help before getting frustrated or complaining to others. This advice is meant to give you some insight into why your child may not yet be able to talk and what you can do about it. By focusing on the positive, you may find more positive things about your toddler's behavior and help them become more comfortable communicating with you.

Parents need to understand what is normal for their toddlers to ensure they create the right environment so their children can talk soon and start learning language skills. It can be frustrating when other children seem able to communicate while you feel nothing is wrong with your child or they are not progressing.

This book aims to provide information, tips, and strategies to help you support your child's language development and address any concerns you may have. It is mainly focused on helping parents and caregivers whose toddler (a child aged 18 to 30 months) is not yet talking or is only speaking a few words. There's no point in rushing your child when they're ready, but this book will give you some things to look out for and watch for.

Remember that every child is unique and develops at their own pace. However, if you feel that your child's language development is significantly delayed compared to other children of the same age, seeking professional help is always a good idea.

This book is intended to be a guide to help you understand your child's language development and provide support to help them grow and thrive. You can help your child reach their full language potential with patience, positivity, and the right resources.

Chapter 1. Understanding Toddler Speech Development

Speech development in toddlers often comes with many frustrations for parents and children alike. They are constantly busy and learning to discuss their often-repeated questions gets old. For parents, having a toddler not talk can be frustrating - especially when they see other little ones on the playground asking their moms or dads questions. Some milestones are the first of their speech development. Some children may be nonverbal briefly but will start acknowledging words by their second birthday.

Many parents may struggle to know when to expect their toddlers to start talking. This can be especially true as it seems as if other people's children are speaking much more than their own. Sadly, there is no natural way to determine when a child will start talking. It is essential for parents and those caring for toddlers to work on speech development but not pressure their little ones to speak at a specific time.

Parents need to be patient and understanding when their children do not start speaking early. However, it may still be helpful for them to contact someone they can talk with about potential speech development issues if they see something wrong or unusual with their speech.

The stages of speech development

One of the many crucial skills that young children develop is the ability to comprehend and communicate through language. Early childhood typically follows a series of steps toward language development, which starts with the early stages of linguistic development in infancy. Although there is no direct correlation between these stages and age, they reflect a pattern or order in how language is learned. These stages of speech development include:

1. Pre-linguistic Stage

This stage includes children that have yet to make any sounds or gestures. At this point, they have not yet grasped the concept of communicating through language.

Infants learn the fundamentals of expressive and receptive language during pre-linguistic speech. Children start using sounds to react to stimuli during this phase of speech development, which lasts for the first six months of an infant's life. These sounds, mainly consisting of cooing and vegetative noises like crying and burping, are just the beginning of the speech. Infants' ability to produce a wide range of sounds is currently somewhat constrained due to the incomplete development of their vocal tracts.

Cooling occurs naturally in the first two months of life, but after that point, around two months, infants can coo on purpose. Children in the pre-linguistic stage can perceive and respond to sounds in receptive language. But at this point, they don't understand what these sounds mean. They can coo, but they don't know why. They are capable of reacting to sounds but not of producing them.

2. Babbling Stage

Children produce more complex sounds not exclusively limited to a single syllable at this stage. They can now mimic sounds from other people, including their parents.

They can now produce more complex sounds that are not exclusively limited to a single syllable, which is known as babbling. Babbling typically begins around nine months but may appear earlier or later depending on the child's physical and neurological development.

Infants begin babbling for all the above reasons: vocal imitation and communication with others. These children make sounds just because they want to communicate with others or themselves, so they don't want to make themselves heard. The child is the one who decides when and how to communicate, which is why babbling comes naturally and frequently. While infants are still working on their vocal bandwidth, this stage of speech development is crucial for further developing receptive and expressive language.

3. One Word Stage

After months of children producing all sorts of sounds without structure or purpose, they combine simple words in meaningful sentences. They learn that certain words go together to make a sentence and can repeat them after their parents or other adults say them.

Children learn that certain words go together to make a sentence during this stage of speech development, which occurs between the ages of one and two. They start using one-word sentences, usually nouns, between their first and second birthdays. Children can say more than one word in a sentence at this point. These utterances often don't make sense as to what the child is trying to say, but they do at least indicate that the child understands concepts such as subject and object.

4. Two-Word Stage

Children begin to string two words together to communicate more significant ideas during this stage of speech development. They may not be able to produce complex language independently, but they can now understand and repeat it once another person has said it.

Children begin to string two words together to communicate more significant ideas during this stage of speech development. This typically starts around the age of two years old. They can now communicate their needs and desires through two-word phrases.

Children use nouns as the first word in their two-word phrases, often related to items they want or need. The second word of these sentences is usually used as an inflectional modifier, expressing things like quantity or tense. For example, a child may ask for "more juice" or state, "I drank it."

5. Telegraphic Stage

At the telegraphic stage, children combine multi-syllable words to communicate their ideas. Most words in their sentences are abstract, indicating a more significant idea rather than referring to objects or people. They can also understand concepts such as time and quantity at this point.

Children's language begins to become more abstract at this stage of speech development between the ages of two and three. They can understand various concepts about space and time at this point. Children may begin using more complex words, such as "day," as meant for "today."

By the age of three, children begin to be able to make more complex sentences. They combine two or more of their one-word sentences into one phrase.

These resulting phrases often include only three words but can consist of various nouns, verbs, and adjectives. Most of these extra words are "function" words, which describe when an action happens or how it is made but don't tell the reader much about what is happening in the sentence.

In addition to these more extended and complex utterances, children start using fewer pronouns and synonyms in this stage of speech development because they no longer need them to communicate ideas.

It's important to note that these stages are just general guidelines, and some children may develop language skills faster or slower than others. Additionally, there may be variations in language development depending on the child's environment, culture, and individual differences.

Parents must be patient and supportive during their child's language development journey. Encouraging communication through play, reading, and talking to your child can go a long way in helping them develop their language skills. If you have concerns about your child's speech development, it's always best to consult a pediatrician or a speech-language pathologist for guidance and support.

Factors that influence speech development

Several factors can influence speech development in toddlers. Some of these factors include:

Age

Infants and toddlers have much more active communication than older children and adults because they cannot filter out background noise or keep their voices within an acceptable volume range for others to hear. They also can't yet understand what is said as children that are two years old can do. This can make talking with them or hearing what they say confusing, which means they need your help and guidance to learn how to speak at this stage of speech development.

Hearing and understanding what your child says to you is one of the most important aspects of speech development. If a child can not know what you are trying to tell them, they will not progress in their language skills.

Environment

The environment where your child is being raised also has a significant impact on their language development as well.

Specific learning environments may make it easier for children to acquire particular skills earlier than others. Also, specific learning environments such as schools, daycare centers, and the home can affect their language development positively or negatively depending on how they are taught and if they learn using more hands-on activities in the classroom.

The environment can also dramatically change what type of words children use when they speak.

Bilingualism

Children exposed to multiple languages may experience a delay in speech development as their brains are processing and learning two languages simultaneously. Although this can occur, it is essential to note that it is relatively short-term, and bilingual children will catch up in their language development within the first few years of life.

Children exposed to multiple languages may experience a delay in speech development as their brains are processing and learning two languages simultaneously. Although this can occur, it is essential to note that it is relatively short-term, and bilingual children will catch up in their language development within the first few years of life.

Language exposure

Children surrounded by people they can communicate with, whether family members or even television characters, will have more exposure to how speech sounds are formed than children who do not have this environment at home. If you are raising a child in a bilingual environment, it is essential to ensure they understand both languages and speak both fluently.

Parenting style

Parenting style can also impact speech development, as parents who talk and interact more with their children may promote language development more effectively. Parents who are more authoritative in their parenting style, setting rules and guidelines that the child must follow but also allowing them to make their own decisions, are more likely to have children with better language skills than those with a much different approach.

Genetics

Genetics can also play an essential role in the way speech develops.

Some children tend to have better speech development. This can be inherited through parents or caused by environmental factors that siblings do not experience.

Genetics can also play an essential role in the way speech develops. Some children tend to have better speech development. This can be inherited through parents or caused by environmental factors that siblings do not experience.

While most children will use a vocabulary appropriate for their age and level of development, those in urban areas or neighborhoods may be exposed to more adult or inappropriate words than children in rural areas.

To have your child develop their language skills quickly, you must ensure they are exposed to the best environment possible. It should be positive and healthy and promote speech development on all levels.

When to expect your toddler to start talking

In general, most toddlers should start to talk around eighteen months of age. Although this is not a strict rule, it is a good guide. If your child appears to have little or no interest in talking, it may indicate they are not ready for the task yet. However, if you are trying hard to get your baby to speak and nothing seems to be working, ensure you don't force them into talking.

Although many factors can influence speech development in toddlers, one of the most important things is being patient and letting them develop naturally without forcing them into speaking too early.

It's important to note that some children may take longer to start talking, which doesn't necessarily mean there is a problem with their speech development. However, suppose a child has not begun talking by 18 months or is not using two-word phrases by two years of age. In that case, it may be a sign of a language delay, and parents should consider consulting with a pediatrician or a speech-language pathologist.

Suppose parents are concerned about their child's speech development at any point. In that case, they can also try to observe other areas of development, such as social interaction, play skills, and non-verbal communication. This can give parents a better idea of whether their child is experiencing a language delay or if there may be other underlying developmental concerns.

Parents need to remember that every child develops at their own pace and not to compare their child's progress to other children. With patience, encouragement, and support, most children will eventually develop their language skills and catch up to their peers. Brain development is a complex process that occurs over several years. Therefore, it is essential to remember that some children will reach milestones at different times than others and not to worry if your child does not develop as quickly as you thought they should.

Chapter 2. Recognizing the Signs of Speech Delays

Speech delay is the term used to describe a child who has not yet developed their vocabulary and speech skills by the time they should have. There are many reasons for this, so it's easy to overlook signs of a possible problem. However, it is essential to be aware of these signs to ensure appropriate early intervention occurs.

Every parent has seen the signs of speech delays in their children. The most basic sign of a delay is when a child does not speak by 2 or 3 years old. Luckily, the signs are more evident than that and start to show when they are slightly older. Speech delays can also be challenging to detect because they can happen outside of speaking and listening, such as when a child gets into trouble at school because they don't understand what's happening.

Parents need to know the symptoms to help them identify if their child is having an issue communicating before too much damage has been done.

Common signs of speech delays

It's important to note that each child develops at their own pace, and some children may experience temporary speech delays that resolve independently. Speech delay often appears around the age of two years old. The following are symptoms of a child having difficulty developing communication skills.

An impulsive child

An impulsive child may not respond to their parents for weeks or months. During this time, the child might voluntarily engage in self-stimulatory behaviors, such as thumb-sucking or rocking back and forth. It's important to note that the behavior of thumb sucking or rocking typically decreases between 18 months and two years old (usually around 15 months).

An impulsive child might engage in these behaviors until they tire of them alone.

An impulsive child might also have a hard time understanding consequences. They may not communicate with others or care when told what happens when they do not follow the rules. This can make it challenging for parents with children with this type of behavior.

Limited vocabulary

Children with speech delays may have a smaller vocabulary than their peers and struggle to learn new words. It is common for children to have their own words or phrases like "gaga" or "yuck," but if they use them exclusively, they may not learn how to use other words correctly.

A child may also have delays in grammar, such as difficulty with the order of words in a sentence. It is also important to note that it's common for children to be unable to say certain sounds until after their second birthday, and many of the problems resolve on their own around ages three and four.

A delayed manner of speaking

Children might speak more slowly than their peers and have trouble learning new words. They may only be able to say a few words at a time and struggle to put words together. A child with a speech delay might also use fewer hand gestures or facial expressions while communicating.

Difficulty with pronunciation

Children with speech delays may struggle to produce sounds correctly, making it difficult for others to understand them.

Children with delays might also have a hard time hearing the difference between similar sounds, such as the difference between the "th" and "d" or "sh" and "ch."

They might also have trouble with sounds not in their native language. Bilingual children may struggle to produce sounds for words in a different language.

Lack of understanding of language

Children with speech delays may misunderstand what other people say because they don't understand how words work together. They commonly use their names or terms to describe things, confusing others. A delayed child will often ask for clarification when talking to others. They may also have trouble keeping a conversation going once it has started.

A speech-delayed child with difficulty understanding language may misunderstand questions and take things literally. They might also understand what someone is saying and pretend not to understand to get out of doing something or get out of trouble.

Difficulty following conversations

Children with speech delays might have a hard time following conversations that are around them or that they don't know about. It is also common for them to have difficulty recognizing other people's sounds.

Difficulty understanding nonverbal signals

A delayed child might be unable to read or understand nonverbal cues, such as facial expressions or gestures. Also, children with speech delays may have difficulty understanding the tone of voice. They might also have difficulty using language because they miss emotional cues and are unaware of how others feel.

Lack of interest in communicating

Children with speech delays may be less interested in communicating with others and may not engage in babbling, cooing, or other vocalizations as much as their peers. They may also avoid eye contact when talking to people and avoid playing with other children. It is typical for a child with a speech delay to be slightly behind in socialization skills.

Some children may choose to play by themselves while they are waiting for peers to catch up with them. The age at which this happens varies among the child, but it is often between the ages of 3 and 24 months old (when most children are learning to speak).

It is usual for a child not to talk as much as their peers, but parents should watch out for those who don't seem interested in playing or communicating.

Cruelty

Some children may act out by throwing temper tantrums. They may be difficult to reason with when angry and in a bad mood, and they might refuse to do things asked of them or when they are told no. They may also have a hard time understanding their emotions and the emotions of others, which can make it challenging for parents to know why the child is acting out.

A cruel child could also exhibit aggressive behavior toward others, including hitting, scratching, or biting.

Difficulty initiating conversation

When asked a question, a child with difficulty initiating conversation may give vague replies or not respond. They might also be described as having a "quiet" personality because they generally do not talk much. This symptom can indicate speech delay as well as autism.

More than three words at 18 months old

A child who is not making more than three words by 18 months old is on the path to developing speech delay. At this point, the child should have several thousand words. Speech delay usually starts around two years old and continues to improve over time.

Playing with toys but not talking or making up phrases

Most toddlers get their first toy by playing with it during this period and then trying to say what they are playing with. A child who does not talk or make up phrases may seem fine while playing with a toy but might have difficulty communicating once they stop or start talking about something else.

Lack of response

If a child is not responding to words or actions but can physically understand what is being said to them, it may be due to a speech delay. It's also possible that the child has autism, so parents and doctors must monitor children with this behavior.

Difficulty following instructions

Children with speech delays may have trouble following instructions, making it difficult to understand what they are asked. They might have difficulty understanding the difference between similar or related words or recognizing and understanding nonverbal signals.

A child with a speech delay usually uses sentence structure that is not expected of their age group, such as "I go wash hands." Parents should be on the lookout for this type of behavior in their children and take action to correct it.

Social withdrawal

Children with speech delays may withdraw from social situations or avoid interacting with others, impacting their social development.

This is because people with a speech delay may not understand social cues well or feel uncomfortable talking to others until they have some experience and understanding. They may have a hard time understanding the emotional state of others, leading them to appear rude or avoidant.

The symptoms of speech delay can be frightening for parents and doctors, but there are ways for professionals to distinguish a speech delay from other conditions. It is difficult for doctors to diagnose speech delay when no signs of autism are present, yet the two conditions seem similar at first glance. Speech delay and autism are not the only conditions that can cause speech problems in children; parents need to watch for other signs.

How to differentiate between typical delays and more severe issues

Parents can struggle to differentiate between typical speech delays and more severe issues.

Here's how you can differentiate between typical delays and more severe issues:

A parent will typically notice that their child has a speech delay by the time they are two years old. They may struggle to understand the emotional state of others, or they may not respond to people when they are being spoken to. They might also be described as having a "quiet" personality because they generally do not talk much. A child will have a vocabulary of over 3,000 words by two years old. That child should also be able to follow simple instructions and respond to them.

A child who does not talk during the day or has a "quiet personality" can sometimes lead doctors to misdiagnose childhood autism. This is why parents need to monitor their child's behavior, so they can identify when the symptoms match those of speech delay or other conditions.

There are two possibilities if a child does not respond verbally, follow instructions well, or show emotion when talking or interacting with others. The first possibility is that the child has autism, so it's essential for parents and doctors to keep an eye on children with this type of behavior. The second possibility is that the child has a speech delay. In some cases, such as when a child seems to be "holding something back" or seems angry but not vocalizing their emotions, they could be experiencing a general communication blockage called receptive language delay.

Children develop language skills at different rates, but there are some general age ranges for speech milestones. If your child is not meeting these milestones, it may be a sign of a speech delay or a more severe issue.

Paying attention to the progression of your child's language development is essential. For example, if your child has a small vocabulary at 18 months but is rapidly acquiring new words, it's likely a typical delay. However, if your child has not progressed in several months, it may be a sign of a more serious issue.

If there is a history of speech or language delays in your family, your child may be at a higher risk for a speech delay or a more severe issue.

Children with a parent with an auditory processing disorder, or hearing-impaired, are at a higher risk for speech delay. Children with speech delays are more likely to have language and related learning problems, such as a lack of motor skills. They are also at risk for emotional and behavioral issues.

If your child has trouble communicating verbally but not through other means, such as sign language or gestures, it could be more than just a typical delay in development. Sometimes, children do not speak until they begin school with others their age, which is known as social communication delay.

If your child consistently uses the same sounds or words or rarely uses language to communicate, it may indicate a delay or disorder. Children with language delays or disorders will struggle to acquire sounds and often struggle to put together words and expressions. They can also have trouble understanding what others are saying to them.

If your child becomes frustrated or upset when they cannot communicate effectively, it may be a sign of a delay or disorder. They may also withdraw from social situations, resulting in symptoms like anxiety or a lack of curiosity.

Children with speech delays are more likely to have learning disabilities because the two conditions can overlap. In addition, children with learning disabilities are often more likely to have language delays and disorders. Children with delays or disorders affecting their ability to learn social skills often have trouble speaking and understanding others.

If you notice that your child has not developed typically, it could be a sign of a delay or disorder causing concern.

Parents need to know the signs of speech delay to distinguish between typical and more severe issues. If you notice language milestones seeming to lag behind those of other children in the same age group, or if your child seems anxious, withdrawn from social situations, or acts frustrated when they cannot communicate effectively, it may be a sign of a delay or disorder.

Language delays and disorders can lead to anxiety, depression, and behavioral issues. If your child has begun to withdraw from friends and family while they struggle with communicating effectively, this is a common sign of a disorder.

When to seek professional help

If you have concerns about your child's speech or language development, it's always best to seek professional help as early as possible. Early intervention is essential for treating speech and language disorders and can help improve your child's communication skills. If a speech delay is left untreated, it can become more severe, resulting in later social problems and other issues. There are several reasons why it's essential to seek professional help before your child experiences more severe issues. It's always best to make an appointment with your child's doctor if you are experiencing any signs of a speech or language delay in your child. If your child is under two, you can call the pediatric office where your child receives treatment.

Here are some signs that may indicate it's time to seek professional help:

1. The child has not progressed in language or communication skills since they began therapy.

2. The child has a habit of speaking gibberish, which is repetitive speech without meaning.

3. The child uses the exact words repeatedly over time or during the day, even if someone asks them to speak about something else. If a child does this, it could indicate an undiagnosed speech delay.

4. Responding to questions and instructions is more complex than usual for your child. This may be due to motor and auditory processing delays.

5. Your child avoids eye contact or appears uncomfortable when faced with strangers, especially other children. This is a sign that your child may have sensory processing delays.

If you have concerns about your son or daughter being able to speak, whether they have just turned two or are five, there are a few things you can do short-term that can help give them the tools they need to speak.

Caring for your child's speech and language development deficit can be challenging. Many parents worry about how to help their child or what's causing the delay. Sometimes, they may also worry that their child will be bullied. The good news is that once a speech and language disorder is caught early, there are ways to treat it and help your child overcome the deficit.

It's important to know that while a speech delay can worsen over time, seeking treatment is never too late. Many children who receive early intervention and one-on-one speech therapy learn to speak just as well as their peers. Many parents report that their speech-delayed children have more empathy for others than children who have not experienced delays. The earlier your child is evaluated and receives treatment for their communication issues, the better the chance that they will be able to develop into a well-spoken adult.

Chapter 3. The Power of Communication: Going Beyond Words

Communication is an integral part of our lives in the 21st century. We rely on communication to express ourselves and exchange ideas as a society. Communication is vital for building relationships, which has become increasingly important with the rise of globalization and technology. Yet children are not born with the ability to communicate effectively; it must be learned as they grow up, starting when they are babies. Although language skills are developed over time, they do not come quickly to children, as discussed in this book. As parents and caregivers, it is essential to remember that communication is a process that begins with non-verbal communication and advances as children transition from infancy to childhood.

Many people think communication is the same as language, but the two concepts differ. Communication refers to our ability to share information through various signs and symbols (words may be one of these symbols; facial expressions and gestures may also be). Language is one of the many ways we communicate, but it is not the only way. Before children learn to speak well, they must first master nonverbal communication.

Importance of non-verbal communication

When children are born, they cannot yet communicate with others in a language sense. However, as a species, people are born with the instinctual need to communicate. This means that infants also need to be able to express themselves, which non-verbal communication fulfills. The ability of infants to communicate through their actions gives them a sense of security; for this reason, parents and caregivers need to pay close attention to their child's non-verbal communication during the early stages of development.

As babies grow older and start talking, they may find their communication skills not as good as they had hoped (perhaps some of you experienced this at one stage). It is easy to expect your child's communication skills to develop like magic, but that is untrue. In some cases, if you do not understand why your child is having difficulty communicating what they want (or why it seems like your child does not know what you are saying), be sure to look at ways in which you can improve your communication skills and help your child along the way.

For parents and caregivers to better assist their children with non-verbal communication, it is essential to look at how babies communicate during their first year of life.

What is the importance of non-verbal communication?

1. Facilitates early communication

Non-verbal communication allows infants to communicate their needs and emotions before they develop language skills. This is important for building strong bonds between caregivers and children.

For example, if a baby is tired, it may become fussy. If the baby continues to cry without any change in facial expression and there is no change in tone of voice, parents, and caregivers will notice this and know that a diaper change is needed. However, if a baby cries with a joyful smile, their parents and caregivers will know that they want to be held. As time passes and children develop language skills, it can be easy to overlook non-verbal communication. However, it is an essential part of child development that should not be ignored because even after children learn to speak well, they continue to rely on non-verbal communication throughout their lives.

2. Enhances language development

Non-verbal communication skills are closely linked to language development. Children good at non-verbal communication are often better at understanding and using language. The ability to communicate via gestures and body language often helps children understand the meaning of words when they start learning to speak. For example, if an infant cries when their mother is saying goodbye as she leaves for work, they may not be able to express their feelings in words but will show that they are upset by crying.

3. Helps children identify emotions

As children transition from infancy to childhood, non-verbal communication allows them to learn about other people's emotions. Infants who can perceive and identify emotions are more likely to develop secure relationships with their parents later in life than other babies (who have trouble recognizing facial expressions).

4. Improves social skills

Non-verbal communication is crucial in social interactions, such as making eye contact, reading facial expressions, and understanding body language. These skills are essential for building and maintaining relationships. For example, if your baby exchanges a look with a parent before grabbing their favorite toy and then walks away, it will be more difficult for the parent to understand what the infant wants. Parents cannot read the child's facial expressions and gestures to determine their wants. However, if an infant smiles at their mother before grabbing and playing with their toy, then holds eye contact while retrieving the toy, and then runs back to play with the same toy again (which means that they understand that mommy is going away), it will be easier for both parties to understand each other.

5. Provides feedback

Non-verbal cues, such as a smile or a frown, can provide feedback to the speaker about how their message is being received. This helps to clarify meaning and can prevent misunderstandings.

6. Enhances development of language skills

A baby's ability to communicate via non-verbal cues is essential for future speech development. As infants pick up language skills, they often refer back to how they communicated before learning to speak (using non-verbal communication). For example, babies who can yawn during feeding will more often than not follow up with the word "mama."

7. Helps parents understand their child

It is not as easy for parents to understand their children as it is for the children to understand their parents. Non-verbal communication often helps to bridge this gap. For example, suppose a baby cries because they are tired. In that case, it may be difficult for a parent to know what the baby wants unless they can figure out that the infant communicates an emotional need through their actions and facial expressions.

8. Supports cognitive development

Non-verbal communication helps infants develop cognitive skills, such as memory and problem-solving, by learning about cause-and-effect relationships.

Non-verbal communication is an essential aspect of early childhood development. Paying attention to your child's non-verbal cues and providing opportunities to practice these skills can help support their overall communication and cognitive development.

Encouraging gestures and signs

While some children are naturally more skilled at using their bodies to communicate, others may need help getting started.

Approaching your baby positively is the first step in encouraging your child to use gestures and signs. It is also essential that you do not expect too much from your baby too soon. Gaining confidence takes time; encouraging it early on will come more naturally as they grow older.

If you do not see a particular sign or gesture for several weeks, remain calm and try new ways of encouraging this form of communication with your infant. This can help to increase your child's ability to communicate, as well as help you both develop and grow together.

Gaining confidence takes time; encouraging it early on will come more naturally as they grow older.

Encouraging your baby's first signs and gestures can be both enjoyable and enriching for the entire family by:

You can ask for help with encouragement from other individuals close to your child, such as a grandparent or a babysitter. But remember that although they are there to make your child happy, it is ultimately up to you as the parent to support their development by encouraging nonverbal communication.

Play with your baby to help them become comfortable using these gestures and signs. For example, if your child is used to taking them out in a stroller, you could gently pull them out and place them beside the crib while leaving the room. When you return to see that your baby has not moved, encourage them by saying something like: "Baby's sleeping; go get our milk when he wakes up." This will encourage your child to use a non-verbal gesture by mimicking eating something (such as a bottle) when they wake up.

Making it a game

If you have friends or family with children the same age as your baby, you can play a "sign game" to help your child learn how to make signs. For example, when other babies sign "food," you might let your toddler guess what they mean by pointing out all the jars of food in their house. This helps your child to recognize words and develop a sense of humor about their baby's language skills.

Ask for help from other individuals who are close to your child. For example, a babysitter or family member is perfect for this exercise.

Creating an environment where your child feels comfortable expressing their needs without being frustrated is essential to develop non-verbal communication.

Be patient and flexible: children take time to learn new skills. Remember that you are the one who will be communicating with your child for many years to come, so try not to feel frustrated or upset when your child does not understand what you want.

As a parent, it can be challenging to interpret your baby's attempts at non-verbal communication. Pay attention to their body language and facial expressions while engaged in this activity to determine whether or not your infant is saying "no" in response to an activity. If the movement was previously enjoyed, they might become upset as soon as it begins. However, if your infant is tired of the activity and would like some time on their own, they may respond by becoming bored and unresponsive.

In general, babies respond best to soft voices; this is because loud voices tend to seem threatening. Therefore, speaking calmly and avoiding raising your voice while interacting with your baby is essential.

Fostering emotional connections

In addition to helping your baby express their needs, encouraging non-verbal communication can also help you and your child to develop a sense of attachment.

By expressing your love through actions, such as smiling and cooing, you allow your child to feel safe and secure when they are with you. The more confident they are in communicating with you, the more likely they are to feel dependent on you and the less likely they will be able to cope with separation anxiety.

The more confident they are in communicating with you, the less likely they will be able to cope with separation anxiety.

Suppose you can recognize when your child is about to become upset. In that case, you can incorporate a word or phrase in the middle of your conversation that relates to their particular stage of development. By using this language, you can help them cope with any impending stress they might be feeling.

For example, a six-month-old baby may respond most effectively to "Here we go again" because it reminds them of the fun moments they had together in the past and when they were starting to walk.

You can even use this method for older children who are no longer babies. For instance, if a toddler is getting upset with you because they have some freedom and autonomy in the house (they have been playing video games rather than doing their chores), you may be able to tell them: "Every time we have fun, Mommy gets scared that you'll get too independent." This will help your child understand that a good relationship needs balance and encourage them to continue being a good helper around the house.

It is essential to be sensitive to your child's needs at each stage of development. For example, if you teach a toddler how to sign "more," wait until they are nearing the end of a meal and then begin making gestures similar to eating more food. This approach allows them to feel full and eat some of their meal before it runs out.

Emotional connections with your toddler are essential for their overall development and well-being. Emotional connections help children feel safe, secure and loved, which is necessary for their social, emotional, and cognitive growth. Here are some tips for fostering emotional connections with your toddler:

Be present and attentive: Children feel connected when they receive your undivided attention. Spend quality time with your child, listen to their stories, and show genuine interest in their world.

Show affection: Physical touches, such as hugs and cuddles, can help to strengthen the emotional bond between you and your child. Remember to show affection through words and actions, as well.

Be responsive: Respond with empathy and understanding when your child expresses emotions. This helps them feel heard and validated, which builds trust and strengthens your connection.

Share in their interests: Take an interest in what your child likes to do and join in with their play. This shows your child that you value their interests and strengthens your relationship.

Be consistent: Consistency is critical when it comes to building emotional connections. Be consistent in your words and actions, and follow through on promises. This helps to build trust and a sense of security.

Every child is unique; building emotional connections takes time and effort. By showing your child love, attention, and consistency, you can help to foster a strong emotional connection that will benefit them throughout their lives.

Chapter 4.   Setting the Stage for Speech

This refers to creating an environment conducive to a child's speech development. It provides opportunities for your child to practice their communication skills and build their vocabulary through interactions, play, and other activities. By setting the stage for speech, you can help your child develop their language skills and improve their ability to communicate with others. This can include activities such as reading to your child, talking to them throughout the day, providing opportunities for play, and limiting screen time. It is important to remember that every child develops at their own pace, and it may take time and patience to see progress in their speech and language skills.

Creating a language-rich tremendous

A language-rich environment includes a variety of communication possibilities for your child. To see tremendous success in their speech development, provide opportunities for communication through play and games. When reading to your child, point out pictures, ask questions, and discuss the text. If possible, include another adult or older sibling as another interactive voice. This helps build a healthy relationship between you and your children while improving their speaking skills.

How do you create a language-rich environment?

Creating a language-rich environment is a crucial aspect of setting the stage for speech in children. It involves providing an environment where the language surrounds children, allowing them to practice and develop their communication skills.

Here are some tips for creating a language-rich environment:

Expand expressive language. Use gestures, such as pointing or waving, to expand babies' early communication skills. As they age, please encourage them to communicate their needs through words and phrases. By giving them the words you want them to say, you are helping them understand that words can be used to communicate. When they begin using one or two-word phrases, follow up with questions that will continue to expand their expressive speech

Expand receptive language. Responding to your child and understanding what he is communicating improves his receptive language skills. This includes repeating what he says, using the same tone of voice, and using body language such as nodding or smiling when he does something correctly. To encourage his verbal interactions, try to avoid correcting him when he makes a mistake and instead focus on understanding what he is trying to say.

Develop speech and language skills with books: Reading to and with your child is a great way to help expand his language skills. The more you interact with your child through books, the more likely you'll be able to help him learn new words, sentences, and play skills. Some ways you can maximize book time include:

Talking while looking at the pictures in the book: Talk about different people/things/places in the pictures and ask questions about them (where are they going? What are they doing? etc.). Point out objects that can be found at home or in the environment.

Talking about what your child is reading: Talk about different parts of the book (such as story, characters, and setting) and ask questions like "What do you think will happen next?" "Who will you be meeting?" etc.

Looking at the pictures yourself: Point to different things in the pictures and ask questions like "What is this? What color is it? What shape is that?"

Develop speech and language skills with play. While using play to express their needs may seem counter-productive, it can help encourage your child's speech development. By playing with toys, interacting with other children and adults, and having conversations with him throughout the day, you are providing opportunities for him to practice speaking.

Provide opportunities for talking. While play can provide opportunities for language development, depending on the child's age, it may not always be appropriate for them. It is essential to monitor your child's play patterns, and if he is using toys or other objects to try and talk, you should encourage him by allowing him to speak. It is also essential to understand that different children take different approaches when playing with toys and other objects. Some younger children may be unable to talk with toys or only use familiar words like mama, puppy, etc. In comparison, older children can typically have more extended conversations about everyday topics such as family members, pets, and specific things like vehicles or foods.

Have conversations throughout the day. Have conversations with your child during the day, and make sure you talk about more than just what he did that day. Talk about general and everyday topics such as family members, favorite toys, subjects of interest, etc. By talking to your child throughout the day, you encourage him to use his words to communicate through play and other activities. If he is not conversing with you during the day, check back later in the evening, as most children will start to communicate more when they are tired and ready for bed.

Use words correctly. When practicing or encouraging speech, your child must use correct language throughout their interactions with you. For example, encouraging your child to use their name instead of saying "mommy" or "daddy" is incorrect. Remember that it is essential for children to learn what is correct and inappropriate language, so make sure you use good communication skills when giving feedback about their speech and language.

Play with your child. Children learn best through play, and their language skills are no different. Play with your child creatively, encouraging them to use their words and other communication skills. For example, ask your child what he is doing with the toys or if he can help you find something in the house. When interacting with him, allow him to talk freely and try different things out of curiosity.

Limit screen time. While no magic number indicates an appropriate amount of time to spend watching television or being on the computer, monitoring how much your child spends on these electronic devices is crucial. Although electronic toys can encourage children's language skills, much television and computer time can discourage it. This can happen because they are not interacting with others, not using all of their senses, and lack imagination.

Your child's language development is shaped by his environment and interactions with people, objects, and places. By creating a language-rich environment for your child that encourages him to use his words, you are helping him develop his communication skills early.

Encouraging imitation and repetition

When children imitate other people, they learn how to use the words and sentences of others. Encouraging imitation during early childhood can significantly improve a child's receptive language skills. This is especially true for young children who cannot know what others are saying, so a child can learn new language skills by hearing and seeing things done by others; a ch Often, for children who have difficulty talking, there is some form of latency or delay in their development, which means that they cannot know or understand all of their words as they should by their first birthday.

Children learn best through multiple sensory stimulations, including sight, sound, touch, and movement. Children learn words and language best when they imitate and repeat what others do in their environment.

Imitation and repetition are essential tools for speech development in young children. Encouraging your child to imitate and repeat words and sounds can help them learn new words, develop their articulation, and improve their speech fluency. Here are some tips for encouraging imitation and repetition:

Model language

One of the easiest and most effective ways to help your child learn new words is to model them. When talking with someone or playing with a family member, ask your child questions about what you are doing or say the names of people, places, or things you see. This will allow your child to imitate the words and sentences he hears to learn them. Use clear, simple, correct language to be a good language model for your child. Repeat words or phrases to emphasize their meaning.

Use gestures

Encouraging imitation of gestures can benefit children's language skills as well. Gesticulation is using the hands, facial expressions, and body movements to communicate meaning and enhance speech. Gestures such as pointing is a good way for your child to understand many familiar words and phrases, such as "over there" or "more."

Babies learn most words and sentences by hearing them spoken by others in their environment and seeing them in books, movies, and television. Your child can model these words in multiple ways, including talking, pointing, singing, and imitating facial expressions.

Encourage play and pretend play

Pretend play among children can be good for helping them learn more words. This is because pretend play allows them to play out situations they have heard about from their environment and encourages them to use words and other language skills. This includes gestures, facial expressions, and proper sentence structure. For example, if your child plays with a friend, he can make his friend "sit down" because he has seen you do this often.

Use pictures

Pictures can also be great for helping your child learn new words and language skills. Using simple objects or pictures on flashcards is an excellent way to help your child learn new words by connecting the picture with the word you say when showing it to him. This will encourage your child to use words to describe what he is seeing.

Slow down

Sometimes when talking to others, it is easy to forget that young children struggle with understanding and saying words correctly. This is why it is best to slow down and talk more clearly when talking to your child. A slower pace allows children to understand what you are saying and allows them time to say the words correctly.

Encouraging conversations with parents

Children learn new language skills through interactions with others, especially those closest to them, such as parents. When you are interacting with your child, make sure that you give him an opportunity for conversation about what he sees, does, or feels. This can help him learn new words and sentence structure.

Repeat words and sounds

Repeat words and frequent sounds to help your child remember them. You can also encourage your child to repeat words after you or to say a word that rhymes with the word you just said. For example, if you ask your child how to pronounce a particular word or what it means, you can encourage him to repeat the word after you.

Use rhyming words in sentences

Encouraging rhyming is an excellent way for children to learn new words because they enjoy this, and it's fun. For example, if you want your child to say "blah," ask him "blah-loo" because this rhymes with the word "play." You can encourage your child to say the same thing differently by saying "no like" or "not much."

Read aloud

Reading books aloud to your child can allow them to hear and repeat new words. For example, when reading aloud to your child about a pet, ask him about the animal's name. When reading a story to your child, attach each word or sentence with a picture in their mind of what it means by making sounds.

Do not rush your child when he is trying to talk. Instead, let him practice his words and sentence structures until he has them down perfectly. This will allow him to develop new vocabulary and better language skills.

Getting down at eye level with your child is also a good idea when interacting with him. This way, he can see your facial expressions, gestures, and body language while you talk to him to understand each other better.

Include both written and spoken language in any communication that goes on between you and your child. He can hear both types of communication and see pictures representing words or concepts he does not understand. This will make it easier to use more complex words for simple ideas and vice versa for your child to become more independent. Please encourage your child to learn words through their use in books and games. This will give your child a more comprehensive vocabulary for understanding new concepts and help them know what they see, hear, and do in their world. Learning the definition of words can be even more fun for children when combined with role-playing, games, or reading stories involving new vocabulary and hands-on activities such as building blocks.

Remember, children learn through repetition and practice. Encouraging imitation and repetition can help your child develop their language skills and become more confident communicators. By starting in the early stages of language development and navigating through these stages, your child can communicate more effectively and be more independent.

Using simple acting skills such as acting out what you are saying or acting out situations that you see and hear, your child can practice using new words to do this and have fun doing it simultaneously. This helps children understand the words they are learning and practice sentence structure.

Using age-appropriate toys and activities

Using age-appropriate toys and activities in your child's environment is essential. This is because they will learn more effectively through play when engaging with toys that match the skill level of their developing language skills. Try to create a learning environment that is fun and has things that your child finds interesting. For example, if you want your child to learn about numbers, make sure he can interact with a toy or activity involving numbers, such as puzzles, drawing different shapes, and playing games.

Using age-appropriate toys and activities can also play an essential role in fostering speech development in young children. Here are some tips for selecting age-appropriate toys and activities to support language development:

Choose toys that encourage communication

Select toys encouraging children to communicate and interact with others, such as dolls, stuffed animals, and pretend play sets. Play with them and talk to them out loud or in sign language. This helps children to develop their communication skills and make role-playing activities more exciting and fun.

Watch your child while they are playing

Watch your child while they have a playtime activity. Children can have different interests simultaneously, so choose an age-appropriate move for your child's interests. However, ensure you do not influence your child's choices by pressuring him to play with toys or use specific objects. They should be doing this because they want to learn more about it and enjoy it. This can help children learn faster due to their desire to do so.

Use educational toys

Choose toys designed to teach children about language, such as alphabet blocks or shape sorters with words or pictures on them. This can encourage your child to be more aware of new words and concepts and help them learn about them.

Select developmentally appropriate toys

You may want to choose a more developmentally appropriate toy for your child's age. This will help guide you in the type of play you want your child to engage in and what you may want him to learn from it. For example, children under two should not use toys with small parts or sharp edges, such as pencils or scissors. A toy with small parts smaller than 1 inch or 3 cm is considered too dangerous for young children. Depending on your child's age, you may also have restrictions on certain types of toys. If you have children under two years of age, you cannot buy toys with small parts.

Encourage creativity

Art supplies, building blocks, and other open-ended toys can encourage children to use their imaginations and express themselves in new ways. This will help them learn new words, develop their language skills, and expand their vocabulary.

Many toys and activities can help children learn new words, but the key is to choose ones that are age-appropriate for your child. Select toys that focus on appropriate developmental skills, but do not pressure your child to play with specific toys. Help them learn by playing with them and positively interacting with them.

Remember, children learn best through play and exploration. By providing age-appropriate toys and activities, you can help your child develop their language skills in a fun and natural way.

Chapter 5. Six-Week Plan for Getting Your Toddler to Start Talking – Overview

A six-week plan is a structured program to help parents or caregivers support their toddler's speech development over six weeks. It typically includes specific activities, strategies, and goals to work on weekly to improve the child's communication skills and encourage them to start talking. The six-week plan is intended to provide a clear roadmap for parents to support their child's language development systematically and effectively.

Among the most commonly used tools to support toddlers' speech development, a six-week plan is structured so parents or caregivers can follow a manageable and organized path to improving their child's communication skills.

They do this by working with their child daily on specific goals, activities, and plans carefully selected and developed to move communication along. This allows parents to work towards increasing their child's language skills and encouraging them to start talking while also helping them to solve any problems they might have with the ability to talk.

The tool described here is one of the most commonly used programs designed to help toddlers learn how to speak. In addition, it is one of the most effective at helping parents or caregivers see a rapid improvement in their child's communication skills and reducing behavior issues associated with not speaking. Many toddlers who can communicate within a few weeks of participating in a six-week program will significantly increase their daily interactions and play. As a result, most parents and caregivers of these children report that their child's mood and overall behavior have improved significantly.

In addition to providing a detailed description of a six-week program, this book also describes the most common concerns parents or caregivers of toddlers have about their child's speech development. It then provides suggestions for how they can get started and how to work with their toddler throughout the six-week program.

Introduction to the 6-week plan

The 6-week plan for increasing your child's ability to communicate is one of the most effective aids at helping many toddlers to develop their ability to speak. It is a structured plan developed over the years by a team of speech-language pathologists, child development experts, and parents dedicated to providing children with the best language skills possible.

The program was initially intended for children who had not yet started talking during the first year of life. However, there are programs for children as young as three months of age that can help them establish communication and start processing language more quickly than they would otherwise be able to do on their own.

As a result, the importance of the 6-week plan cannot be overstated. It is a structured program that helps children model the skills they will be developing and encourages them to use them whenever and wherever possible to improve their communication ability. It is also intended to support parents in teaching their children how to talk more quickly than they could if left alone.

Here is an overview of a six-week plan for getting your toddler to start talking:

Week 1: Building Vocabulary

We will focus on building your toddler's vocabulary during the first week. We will provide tips and activities for introducing new words to your child, using repetition and context to help them understand the meanings of words, and encouraging them to use new words in their speech.

Week 2: Encouraging Imitation and Repetition

In the second week, we will discuss the importance of imitation and repetition in speech development. We will provide you with strategies for modeling language for your child, using games and activities to encourage repetition, and reinforcing your child's attempts to imitate new words and sounds.

Week 3: Engaging in Conversation

During the third week, we will focus on engaging your toddler in conversation. We will provide tips for asking open-ended questions, using wait time to encourage your child to respond, and using play to stimulate discussion.

Week 4: Practicing Pronunciation

In the fourth week, we will provide strategies for helping your child practice pronunciation. We will discuss the importance of phonics and provide you with activities to help your child improve their articulation.

Week 5: Reading and Storytelling

During the fifth week, we will focus on the importance of reading and storytelling in speech development. We will provide tips for choosing age-appropriate books, engaging your child in storytelling, and encouraging them to use their imagination and creativity.

Week 6: Creating a Language-Rich Environment

Finally, during the sixth week, we will discuss the importance of creating a language-rich environment for your child. We will provide tips for using everyday experiences to stimulate language development, creating opportunities for your child to hear and use language, and building your child's confidence in their ability to communicate.

By following this six-week plan, you will take proactive steps to support your child's language development and help them build the necessary skills to start talking. Remember to have fun, stay positive, and celebrate your child's progress!

Tips on how to get started on a 6-week plan

1. Plan ahead

Plan by determining which activities you want to work on at home and how to improve the activity.

As a result, you should have a list of goals and activities you want your child to perform each day. You will also need to equip yourself with the skills necessary for working with your child so that you can provide feedback for improvement and offer encouragement during any difficulties.

And even though the six-week plan will not teach your child about words, it does include exercises that address several of the areas in which goals are being worked on for parents or caregivers to help their child learn new skills, such as listening and responding correctly or saying one word at a time.

2. Introduce the plan to your child

Introduce the six-week plan to your child by explaining what you will do each day and how working on these things will help them improve their communication ability.

3. Each day, follow the plan

Each day, follow the 6-week plan by working on one activity from the previous day and then trying a new move from the current week. If you have already completed an activity, try again by working on it from another angle, such as increasing its length or changing its complexity so your child can learn more.

4. Repeat the plan for six weeks

Repeat the program for six weeks to build on your child's developing ability to communicate. This structured plan must be followed each day so that you can follow a consistent and organized path toward improving your child's speech and language skills.

5. Continue at home

Continue working with your toddler after the six-week program by working on the same goals and activities you have worked on as part of this program. For the best results, continue working with your child for a few months after the program has ended.

The 6-week plan is designed to have parents or caregivers participate in every activity daily while encouraging children with as much practice as possible as they work towards improving their communication skills. However, it is essential to note that the program is not intended to be used by parents who are entirely new to supporting their toddler's language development. For example, if they have not taught their child how to talk, they need more than the six-week plan to help them learn how.

The goal of a six-week program is to improve communication skills. This can include anything from helping children add one word at a time for things like "milk" or "fire," or it can consist of how many words children can use in different situations (such as being in a restaurant or at the park).

Remember, this plan guides and supports you and your child. Every child develops at their own pace, so don't worry if your child doesn't hit every milestone right on schedule. The most important thing is to stay positive, have fun, and enjoy this exciting time in your child's life.

Weekly goals and expectations

The infant program aims to engage your baby in fun activities to encourage motor and language development. The main objective of this stage of development is for them to build up their muscle strength and coordination, so they can practice movements that are at their level. I will provide tips for helping your baby learn to coordinate their activities and work on developing muscle control while stimulating language development and promoting early learning skills like imitation.

1. Weekly Goals

The toddler program aims to help your toddler communicate using various means, such as gestures, vocalizations, sounds, and more. We will provide tips on supporting this process by encouraging your child's communication attempts during playtime. For example, if they point to a toy while saying the word "up," you can model this behavior by pretending to pick up the toy while speaking, "Up!"

We recommend working on one skill at a time for the best results. By working on one skill each day, you can focus specifically on that skill without worrying about remembering everything your child has learned up to that point. Each week of this 6-week program builds upon the previous week's activities so your child can continue developing their skills as long as possible.

2. Weekly Exercises

The exercises below are designed for parents and caregivers working with their infant or toddler at home. They are based on basic daily activities you can do with your child.

Week 1:

Introduce five new words and repeat them regularly throughout the day.

Encourage your toddler to imitate the words and use gestures to help them understand the meaning.

Focus on modeling correct pronunciation and expanding on your child's communication attempts.

Week 2:

Please increase the number of words to 10 and repeat them throughout the day.

Use different types of toys and objects to introduce new vocabulary.

Encourage your toddler to use the words in simple phrases, such as "more milk" or "play ball."

Week 3:

Add five more words to the vocabulary list, focusing on verbs and action words.

Practice following simple directions with your child, such as "Come here" or "Give me a hug."

Use books and songs with repetitive phrases to help your child learn new words.

Week 4:

Expand the vocabulary list with ten more words, including descriptive words.

Use playtime to encourage your child to describe objects and actions.

Read books with more complex sentences and encourage your child to ask questions and make comments about the story.

Week 5:

Introduce pronouns and possessive words, such as "mine" and "yours."

Practice turn-taking in conversation and encourage your child to ask and answer simple questions.

Use rhyming games and songs to help your child learn new words and improve their phonological awareness.

Week 6:

Expand the vocabulary list with ten more words, including prepositions and conjunctions.

Encourage your child to use longer sentences and tell simple stories.

Practice conversational skills, such as listening and responding appropriately to others and taking turns speaking.

3. Practice

In each week of this program, you will have many chances to practice the skills your child has learned. Here are some examples:

At home or daycare, act out the same activities we provided, and be sure to use correct speech and gestures.

Play games with your child in the car that features words and phrases they know.

In the crib, please encourage your child to imitate words they already know by describing objects and actions.

When you go grocery shopping or out for ice cream, introduce new words describing what you buy or eat.

If possible, try to make your daily interactions with others around your home more interactive than they usually would be while working on this plan.

4. Subgoals

To keep your child progressing over the six weeks, try to set up a meeting with your child's doctor or pediatrician if you have any concerns about their development or if you notice any changes that seem unusual for your child. They may also be able to provide you with extra support if they see any other issues (such as adverse reactions or early signs of developmental delays).

Overall, the goal of this program is for parents to build on their child's current ability by encouraging communication attempts during playtime and modeling correct pronunciation. Over the six weeks, we will focus on exercising your child's comprehension skills by reading books and playing games together.

By learning new words, phrases, and communication methods, parents allow their children to continue growing and developing over the long term. Therefore, a secondary goal of this program is to help parents feel comfortable with their child's current level of development and support them if they notice anything unusual.

5. Rewards

Your child's main reward will be the confidence they develop when they understand new words and can use them to communicate. Your toddler may also benefit from seeing you more engaged in their activities, making them feel more confident in their abilities.

The six-week plan outlined above is designed to help parents develop a daily routine where their toddlers can learn new words and communicate in new ways. When toddlers use language, they can participate in many fascinating activities and communicate with others in meaningful ways. This program is also designed to help parents implement a plan they can use again. By learning more words and practicing more conversational skills, toddlers develop their communication skills over time and become better at using them in different situations. Therefore, parents must continue practicing these activities after six weeks so their child can keep developing for as long as possible.

Whether your child is just beginning to form sentences or can't combine two words at once, this six-week program will help them develop their language skills.

Chapter 6. Week 1- Building Vocabulary

Whether you are a parent or an educator, ensuring your toddler builds the vocabulary they need to communicate is essential. This can be done through reading picture books, singing songs that have descriptive words, and listening to podcasts with everyday language. There are also various apps for smartphones that parents can download for their little ones to listen to and touch screens interactively.

Building vocabulary is an early goal and will help your child develop communication skills. When we first begin learning a language, we are exposed to simple words that tell us the name of people, places, and objects. We can string these words together with time to tell a story or give more detailed instructions. Early language development lays the foundation for future years when children verbally express themselves daily.

Introducing new words

Introducing new words early will allow your toddler to learn new things. For example, knowing the terms for visiting people makes it easier for your child to say which friend is coming over and when. They can also begin to understand and use descriptive words in their ways.

How do you introduce new words?

Books

Books can be a fun way to introduce new words and phrases to your child. When reading to your toddler, discuss the story and how the characters feel. Ask them what they think of the main characters and why. This will help them understand sentence structure and begin creating their own stories with their ideas. You can also make up your own stories depending on your setting. Take your child to the local park and describe what's around them.

You can also make homemade books with your toddler. Cut out pictures from magazines and glue them onto construction paper book pages, then allow your toddler to create a story about what's happening in each picture. Allowing your child to use their imagination will help them understand new words and ideas and stimulate their creativity.

Songs

Songs are a fun way for toddlers to learn new words and phrases, especially when they get to sing along. Singing out loud with your toddler helps them learn new words by associating the word with the song's tune. This can be done as a family since children enjoy singing along to many parts of a song. Singing with your toddler also ensures they are singing from their heart and not just memorizing a list of words to perform.

When choosing songs for your toddler, you want to find ones with descriptive words and ones that are interactive, such as Chicka Chicka Boom Boom or ABC of Asking Questions. These will help your child learn how language works, which will help them when they start learning formal languages later in life.

When singing along with your toddler, avoid the typical nursery rhymes. These tend not to have the exact detailed words that would stimulate your child's imagination. Instead, sing songs with an exciting story, such as "Camptown Races"; this song will help teach your child the place names of different towns in America.

Podcasts

Podcasts and audiobooks provide a fun way to learn new words and phrases. They can also be beneficial in teaching conversational skills and helping explain concepts. Podcasts help keep your toddler's interest in learning new words and phrases because they can learn by simply listening.

Audiobooks are a great way to introduce literature to your child and help them expand their vocabulary. Take your child to the library and pick out audiobooks describing different scenes or events. This will help stimulate your child's imagination while they listen to someone else tell them the story.

Creating language-rich environments

When creating an environment for your toddler, select toys with solid descriptive words. This will allow your toddler to see, touch, and hear the new words you want them to learn. The more senses you can stimulate in your toddler, the easier it will be for them to understand and learn new words.

Multicultural toys are a great way to introduce your toddler to different places, people, and phrases. This will help your child understand that different cultures live their lives differently. Encouraging them to play with multicultural toys will also teach them how other people speak and act when they are in their own homes.

Creating language-rich environments can begin at home, but it doesn't stop there! Selecting suitable toys while shopping is critical in helping build a child's vocabulary. When going to the supermarket or another public place, take some time to discuss what you see around you with your toddler. For example, you can discuss the different fruits and vegetables you see while shopping.

The more you expose your child to language, the easier it will be for them to grasp its meaning. This is why incorporating language into everyday activities, such as reading books, singing songs, and playing with toys, is essential. Children who use expressive language daily tend to have higher language skills and better nonverbal communication skills.

Repetition

One of the best ways to introduce a new word to your baby is through repetition. The more times they repeat a word or phrase, the better they will learn and remember it. For example, when introducing the word "dog," one method would be to say the first syllable "doe" and then spell dog by pointing at an object shaped like a dog. You can also try to tell the entire word at a time or sing a song about dogs. By doing this, you are allowing your baby to find the meaning in the word.

Exposing your baby to new words and phrases daily is one of the best ways they can learn. Try incorporating new language into everyday activities and create a rich vocabulary and language environment. This will help your child grasp the meaning of their world and begin their first steps towards learning different languages!

Labeling objects and actions

Labeling objects can help children learn more about the world around them. This also helps with speech development by allowing your child to properly understand how to use words.

It's essential to use the same word consistently when labeling an object so they can better understand the meaning of the language. For example, looking at a chair, you would say "chair" instead of "seat." Using different words for the same object can confuse children, making them not understand what something is called. This is known as synonymy, widespread between parents and their young children.

When labeling an object with your toddler or child, describe it correctly. For example, if you're going to the zoo, you would say, "We're going to the zoo. We are going to see a lion."

Using descriptive words is essential when teaching actions so your child can better understand the movement. For example, when you want your baby or toddler to eat their new food, say, "Open wide!" or "Let's give it a try!". These will help spark your child's curiosity and excite them to try new things.

Labeling objects can help children learn more about the world around them. Using descriptive words and phrases is essential when introducing a new object or action to your baby. Doing so will help spark their curiosity in the things surrounding them and better enable them to utilize language to understand the meanings of life. Try to incorporate labeling objects throughout your day. When you're out and about an exotic location, instead of pointing at the different things around you, try to label each one while describing them.

Labeling objects and actions is a great way to promote language development in young children. Here are some tips for labeling objects and actions:

Start early: You can start labeling objects and actions as early as infancy. Even though your child may not understand the words at first, they will eventually learn to associate the words with the objects and actions.

Use simple words: Use simple words that your child can understand. For example, instead of saying, "Can you hand me the remote control?" you can say, "Remote."

Repeat often: Repeat the names of objects and actions often. Repetition helps your child remember and associate the words with the things and activities.

Point to the object or action: When you label a thing or action, point to it so your child can see what you are talking about.

Use descriptive words: Use descriptive words to help your child understand the object or action. For example, instead of saying "Car," you can say "Red car."

Label actions: Labeling actions are just as crucial as labeling objects. For example, you can say "Jump" or "Run" when playing with your child to label their actions.

Children learn through play and exploration, so labeling objects and actions during playtime can be a fun and effective way to promote language development.

Utilizing everyday activities

Utilizing everyday activities means using the exercises and routines of daily life as opportunities to promote learning and development in young children. For example, cooking, shopping, walking, or doing household chores can teach children new vocabulary, concepts, and skills. By incorporating language-rich activities into these everyday routines, parents and caregivers can help children build their language skills, cognitive abilities, social skills, and other essential developmental skills. The idea is to turn everyday activities into learning experiences that are fun, engaging, and meaningful for children and to help them develop the skills they need to succeed in school and life.

Utilizing everyday activities is a great way to promote language development in young children. Here are some tips for using daily activities to encourage language development:

1. Use the names of objects: When doing everyday activities with your toddler or child, try to use the words for objects. For example, if you are walking in the park, point at things and describe them to your child. "See that tree? It has Christmas lights!" This will get your child thinking about what they see as they go along. You can also say, "Let's take a picture of this!" as you take a picture of an object with your camera or phone.

2. Use descriptive language: When labeling objects and actions, it's essential to use descriptive language so your child knows what you're talking about. For example, when you want to walk through a forest, say, "The trees are tall. There are lots of birds high in the sky."

3. Turn everyday activities into learning experiences: Utilizing daily activities is a great way to promote language development in young children. Turning simple tasks into learning opportunities can help your child build their language, cognitive, social, and other critical developmental skills. Remember that children learn through play and exploration, so using everyday activities as opportunities to teach them new things will help make learning fun for both of you!

Turning everyday activities into educational opportunities means incorporating language-rich tasks such as pointing out objects and describing actions. Try to integrate language by saying the names of things you see when you're out or doing daily routines with your toddler or child. By doing so, you will be setting them up for success in school and life.

4. Turn chores into opportunities: Making chores fun by labeling objects and actions is an easy way to help your child develop the skills they need to succeed in school and life. For example, when cleaning or washing dishes, say things like, "We're going to wash this plate" or "Let's put the soap into the water." After you say these things, label them by pointing out what you want your child to do.

5. Narrate your activities: Narrating your activities is a great way to label actions and objects around you while also helping your child learn about what you are doing. For example, when cooking with your child, tell them about the ingredients and how to measure them.

6. Give instructions: Giving instructions is another excellent way to label actions and objects around you. For example, when cooking with your child, tell them, "Put the egg in the bowl" or "Open up a jar of baby food." Doing this can help them build their cognitive abilities.

7. Encourage conversation: Utilizing everyday activities is a great way to promote language development in young children. Encouraging conversation with your child can help them develop their communication skills and encourage listening and speaking. Please encourage your child to participate in discussions by asking them open-ended questions. For example, you can ask them about their day or what they want to do next.

8. Read together: Reading together is a great way to promote language development. Choose books that are age-appropriate and have simple, engaging stories. Hold a book and point to pictures as you read. You can also use books as an opportunity to practice vocabulary. For example, if you look at a dog picture, say "dog" and ask your child to do the same. You can build your child's vocabulary and learning skills by discussing books.

9. Be conversational: Everyday activities are another great way to promote language development in young children. For example, when playing a board game with your child, you can discuss what your child is doing in the game. You can also ask open-ended questions to encourage conversation and language development.

10. Use real objects: Utilizing everyday activities is a great way to promote language development in young children. Turning daily tasks into learning opportunities can help your child build their language, cognitive, social, and other essential developmental skills. Real objects are another great way to promote language development in young children. For example, when you are at the park or grocery store with your toddler or child, look around and find real things to talk about (i.e., "Look at that tree!")

11. Encourage imaginative play: Encourage your child to use their imagination during playtime. This can help them develop storytelling and creative thinking skills. This will help them become more creative adults and enhance their imagination, creativity, and creativity skills.

Remember that children learn best through play and exploration, so try to make language development a fun experience for your child. By incorporating language activities into your everyday routines, you can help your child develop strong language skills and prepare them for success in school and beyond.

Chapter 7. Week 2- Encouraging Interaction

Encouraging interaction refers to the actions of parents or caregivers to promote communication and socialization between themselves and young children. Interaction is essential for promoting language development and building social skills in children. Encouraging interaction means creating a nurturing and supportive environment that fosters communication and socialization in young children.

Parents and caregivers can encourage interaction in many ways, such as by talking and playing with their children, responding to their cues, asking open-ended questions, and praising their efforts. They can also create opportunities for their child to interact with others by arranging play dates, attending community events, and participating in group activities.

Encouraging interaction is crucial for a child's overall development and helps build positive relationships with their caregivers. It promotes language development, cognitive development, social-emotional development, and overall well-being. By actively encouraging interaction, parents, and caregivers help their children build the skills and confidence they need to succeed in school and life.

Engaging in conversation

Many parents and caregivers feel inner conflicts about conversing with their children. They worry that their child will be upset if they engage them in conversation, will not understand what they are saying, or will find the interaction boring and annoying. To overcome these fears, many parents have tried to avoid conversation with their children altogether by worrying that if they engage the child in exchange, they will become too attached and upset when the parent has to leave. This is not a logical way to cope with feelings of discomfort around communication with one's child! Parents are simply avoiding the situation that they fear. They must approach the communication situation differently to learn how to best support their child during interaction and communication.

Engaging in conversation involves actively participating in a two-way exchange of ideas, thoughts, and feelings with another person. When conversing with young children, keeping their developmental level and communication abilities in mind is essential. Young children often do not understand or remember much of what parents and caregivers say to them, so communication with toddlers differs from communication with older children. Toddlers are very concrete, literal thinkers. They learn best through actions and sensory experiences rather than language alone.

Children between 18 months and 36 months are learning language skills and how to use their words effectively. Parents and caregivers must help their children develop language skills by interacting with them daily in an interactive way.

Parents do not have to engage in long conversations or use complicated words when communicating with young children. Less is more, and parents can choose words carefully to help their children understand. The key to effective communication is not to speak too much or use complicated grammar but to try to put the child at ease and speak. Encouraging interaction and communication helps children develop responsiveness, which they will use throughout life.

Encouraging interaction, verbal communication face-to-face with your toddler

When encouraging interaction with your toddler, it is essential to have fun with it and make it enjoyable for both you and your toddler. By taking this approach, you can be more relaxed when interacting with your child, making engaging in conversation easier overall.

Encouraging interaction means you can begin interacting with your child while they are still learning the language. The best way to start is by using simple words and phrases that can be repeated. When your child begins to understand the terms and phrases, use longer sentences or talk about more complex ideas.

Encourage your child's interest in learning new words

You do not have to talk only with your child to encourage interaction. By helping them discover new things, you encourage their interest in learning. You can help your toddler learn new words and develop their vocabulary in many ways. For example, you can point out things around the room, in the car, or during a walk and get your child to name them. You can also encourage your child's interest in learning new words by looking at books with her or showing them how to do a particular activity.

Ask questions

When encouraging interaction, ask simple questions requiring short answers and information about your child. For example, ask, "What do you want?" rather than "Tell me what you did today." Try to make one-on-one interactions between yourself and your young child as natural as possible. Do not feel that every interaction has to be a lesson of some type. Encouraging interaction, using dialogue, and talking to your toddler

Learn to use the natural verbal interaction between you and your child daily. You can ask questions while waiting for your child or buying them something. You can also have conversations with your child while they are playing quietly by herself.

Be present and attentive

When conversing with your child, please give them your undivided attention. Avoid distractions like your phone or other devices, and actively listen to your child's words. Do not talk too much; listen to your child's words and respond by offering information, sharing experiences, and giving advice. Do not interrupt or speak over your child to complete a task or get a result. Engaging in conversation

Remember that you are both sharing experiences. When talking with your toddler, you can take turns expressing thoughts and feelings so that they can also participate in the conversation. Children enjoy being listened to and receiving attention from adults, so they will be attracted to conversations with you that are enjoyable for them as well!

Use simple language

Use simple words and sentences that your child can understand. Avoid using complex vocabulary or sentence structures that may be too challenging for them. Try to communicate whatever you want to tell your toddler in a way that does not confuse them.

Use natural stimulation

Talk and interact with your child when necessary for you and enjoyable for them. Please encourage your child's interests by showing excitement about their actions, explaining how something works, or showing emotion.

Be patient

Give your child time to process their thoughts and respond. Avoid interrupting or finishing their sentences for them. Ensure you do not talk to your child too much by repeating what they just said. Do not always correct them in your conversations. Your children will learn how to fix themselves as they get older, but when you are young, it is essential to let them make mistakes on their own. If your child causes an error, apologize and tell them it's okay.

Encourage talking as well as listening

Children must participate actively in conversations with adults. Sometimes when we are telling stories or showing pictures, our children may sit quietly and listen intently, so it can be tempting to turn off the role-play or illustrated book due to this response from our children.

Encourage elaboration

When your child responds to your questions, please encourage them to elaborate and provide more details. This helps to build their language skills and expand their vocabulary.

Praise your children

Language development is fostered by praise and encouragement. When you speak positively about the things that your children do right or tell them how proud of them you are for something that they did, this encourages their confidence and boosts language development.

Encourage physical play and social skills

Children have many physical abilities from which they can choose. This includes upper body strength as well as agility and speed. Your child may be able to manipulate toys and smaller objects, climb on things, or walk. By encouraging these skills, you are giving your child a safe and enjoyable way to try new ways of moving and playing.

As your children grow more confident and gain more physical abilities, they can begin to express themselves through physical play. Physical play is also essential for developing social skills, such as taking turns with other children and interacting with others. Encourage your child's physical play by modeling the type of behavior that you want them to emulate. For example, if you want your child to share their toys with another toddler in the park, take turns playing with the toy yourself.

Provide feedback and positive reinforcement

Please provide feedback to your child to let them know you are listening and interested in what they say. Positive reinforcement, such as praise and encouragement, can help to build their confidence and self-esteem.

Explain what is going on

When communicating with your child, provide information that helps them understand what is happening. This will help you improve your vocabulary, expand your child's knowledge about the world, and develop their analytical skills.

Keep it interesting and exciting

When providing the information, you want your child to pay attention to, keep it interesting by using natural stimulation such as bodily movements or touching. This can help to make your explanations much more enjoyable and memorable for your children!

Maintain eye contact with your children whenever possible. Eye contact will help them learn how to read facial expressions and maintain an understanding of what you are saying. If you are trying to get your toddler's attention, wait until they look at you. Do not try to read your child's mind!

Provide explanations based on what your child can understand at their age level. This can help foster a better understanding of their world and build self-esteem.

Ensure that your conversation is relevant to the context in which it occurs. If it is bedtime, make sure you have a bedtime story planned for the evening! If you are going out for dinner, plan what restaurant will have dinner at them and what will be happening there.

Conversation with young children is crucial for promoting language development and building social skills. By actively listening and participating in discussions, parents and caregivers can help their children develop their language skills, cognitive abilities, social skills, and other essential developmental skills.

Encouraging interaction is a necessary skill that parents and caregivers need to learn how to do for their young children to develop language skills, social-emotional skills, and cognitive abilities. Parents who engage in conversation with their toddlers help promote cognitive development.

Asking open-ended questions

By having open-ended questions, you are helping to improve your child's social skills. Open-ended questions ask your children for more than a yes or no answer. Open-ended questions can help you explore a larger worldview that is similar to the one that your child has! An example of an open-ended question would be: "Why do you think Mommy got the book?" This helps parents and caregivers ask their children about current events in the world and at home, which helps children connect with the present moment.

By asking open-ended questions, adults can build relationships with their children better. This can also promote positive behavior such as cooperation, sharing, or helping others. By asking open-ended questions, parents can evaluate their child's current abilities, follow up on what the child has learned from them, or assess how well a child understands certain information.

By asking open-ended questions, you are helping your children to build vocabulary and expand their knowledge. These questions allow you to understand what your children know about their world. By asking about the things that interest them, you can make those things more enjoyable for your children and allow you to expand their worldview.

If your child has difficulty answering a question, provide support by telling them what information they need to answer the question. This helps your child to understand better the question being asked of them!

When asking open-ended questions, it also helps to use your body animatedly. For example, if you ask, "Who took my keys?" as soon as you walk into the house, point at yourself and your door. If no one is outside your home, but you are confident that someone took your keys, point outside while saying: "I bet they are out there!". This helps your child to recognize and develop their ability to connect symbolic meaning to an image.

Asking open-ended questions is a communication technique that encourages the person you are talking to, especially children, to provide a detailed and thoughtful response. Open-ended questions require more than a simple "yes" or "no" answer and often start with words such as "what," "how," or "why."

Asking open-ended questions can be especially effective when talking to children because it encourages them to think critically and express their thoughts and ideas more clearly. Asking open-ended questions encourages your child to answer with a few words and a detailed description. These benefits children because it helps them express their opinions and thoughts more completely. It also promotes thoughtful conversations between caregivers and children.

By asking an open-ended question, such as "How do you think I should prepare for this activity?" you will understand what your child thinks about that activity. You will be able to gain information about how your child feels about the activity that you have planned.

By asking open-ended questions, you can engage children in conversation, promote language development, and encourage them to think creatively and critically. Open-ended questions can help children build their vocabulary and improve their listening and social-emotional skills.

Praising efforts

Praising can be a way for parents and caregivers to show children how much they value them. Children learn by watching their parents, so when you praise, your child is learning the appropriate response from you. When you applaud your child's effort, they receive positive reinforcement that encourages them to try harder and continue to work hard at what they are doing.

Praise is a positive way to encourage children to keep working hard in all areas of life! Praise helps children feel good about themselves and contributes to their self-esteem. Praising can also help children learn that hard work will eventually benefit them, even if they do not like a specific task. Praising also encourages children to interact socially with people and helps them build their social skills.

Praising toddlers for their efforts can help encourage them to continue to work hard. This can promote continued work on a task that they may not like or find difficult. Praising your child's curiosity helps them to appreciate the world around them. By praising your child when they are imaginative, you are helping them stay curious! This will help them grow as human beings and learn new things in life.

Praising children's attempts at new tasks can make it easier for them to try a recent activity or challenge themselves in other ways. Encouragement from a parent or caregiver is just one way children get the support they need to pursue essential activities.

Raising efforts refers to acknowledging and recognizing a child's attempts and progress, regardless of the outcome. Praising effort rather than just the result can help build a child's self-esteem, confidence, and motivation to continue trying, even when faced with challenges.

Here are some tips for praising efforts:

Be specific: When praising a child's effort, describe what they did well. For example, instead of saying, "Good job," say, "I'm proud of you for working hard on your project."

Focus on progress: Recognize the child's progress rather than the outcome. For example, "I can see how much you have improved your writing skills."

Encourage problem-solving: Praise the child for problem-solving and overcoming challenges. For example, "I saw how you tried different approaches to solve that puzzle, great job!"

Use positive language: Use positive language when praising efforts. Avoid using negative words such as "not bad" or "not terrible," and instead use positive words such as "great" or "fantastic."

Be genuine: Children can often sense insincere praise. Therefore, be genuine in your praise and ensure it is deserved.

Praising efforts can help build a child's confidence and self-esteem, promote a positive attitude toward learning, and encourage them to persevere and try new things. Recognizing a child's hard work and progress is essential, and praise can be an effective way to do so.

Chapter 8. Week- 3 Reading and Storytelling

Reading, telling stories, and singing songs with your child are the most important activities you can do to help him learn to speak. Reading and storytelling are activities that involve reading books or telling stories to children. It consists in reading aloud from a book, while storytelling involves creating and sharing stories orally. Both activities are essential for promoting language and literacy development in children and developing cognitive, social-emotional, and imaginative skills.

When reading or storytelling with children, caregivers can choose age-appropriate books or stories that match the child's interests and reading level. Caregivers can use different voices, gestures, and facial expressions to make the reading or storytelling more engaging and interactive. They can also ask questions, make predictions, and connect the story to real-life experiences to promote comprehension and understanding.

Reading and storytelling can be incorporated into daily routines, such as bedtime or mealtime, to create a regular habit and foster children's love of learning and reading. These activities can also strengthen the bond between caregiver and child and provide a positive and enjoyable way to spend time together.

The importance of reading aloud

Reading aloud to children is essential for developing a love of books and learning. When caregivers spend more time reading with children, it has been shown to improve their language and literacy skills. Reading aloud is an excellent way to model speech and oral language to children, which helps them learn how to speak. It can also help caregivers to develop their writing skills. Reading to young children (18 months and below) allows them to build confidence and make connections between reading and the meaning of words. Reading aloud has increased vocabulary size and word recognition skills in children aged 6–9. It has also been shown that children who read more learn more, especially when they are rewarded with a verbal response from their parent or caregiver when they have read a certain number of books or pages.

Reading aloud is an important activity that can benefit children in many ways. Here are some reasons why reading aloud is essential:

Language development

Reading aloud exposes children to new words, sentence structures, and vocabulary, which can enhance their language development and communication skills. When children hear a new word, they can learn the meaning of the word when their caregivers explain it in context. As children become more familiar with sight words, they can decode and read them by sight instead of sounding them out. Every time parents or caregivers read to children; they can hear and practice the oral language in a social setting.

Reading aloud allows parents to explain the meanings of new concepts and words children encounter throughout the story. It also promotes language development through storytelling by encouraging creativity and imagination in children as they envision characters and settings in their minds. Reading aloud also allows caregivers to model different speech patterns, such as using other voices or paces while reading the book aloud.

Cognitive development

Reading aloud can help children develop critical thinking and problem-solving skills as they make predictions, ask questions, and infer meaning. Reading aloud helps children develop higher-order cognitive abilities by allowing them to compare what they read to what they already know and have experienced. Books with similar themes, characters, settings, and other elements can also help children better understand what they are reading.

Through reading aloud and sharing stories with family members or caregivers, children develop social skills by interacting with different relatives and their voices. Through talking about the characters in their stories, kids learn how to connect the characters' situations and their own experiences. This will help them become more competent listeners in future interactions.

Imagination and creativity

Reading aloud can spark children's imagination and creativity, allowing them to explore different worlds, characters, and scenarios. This can help them develop a sense of humor, better problem-solving skills, and an insight into the experiences of others. It also allows children to think about the meaning of what they have read and understand the significance of a story.

Reading aloud also allows caregivers to guide children's thinking by asking questions and responding to their reactions to the stories to promote children's critical thinking, problem-solving skills, and understanding of themselves and others. When caregivers talk with their children after reading, they can ask questions about what was read or lead them into conversations that expand their imagination and creativity.

Social-emotional development

Reading aloud can help children develop empathy, emotional intelligence, and social skills as they learn about different experiences and perspectives. It also builds self-confidence and feelings of success. As they read aloud to their caregivers, children get more involved in the stories by making predictions and asking questions which can help them gain a sense of pride and accomplishment.

Children learn to recognize their emotions in different situations and develop empathy for characters' emotions through stories. They may be excited or nervous about what will happen next or sad when something terrible happens - all normal responses to a book that may otherwise be hard for children to understand without having this experience.

Reading aloud can help build children's self-esteem by listening to their caregivers praise them for reading well or asking questions about the story.

Bonding and connection

Reading aloud allows caregivers and children to bond and connect over a shared experience, promoting a positive relationship and a love of learning. When caregivers read to a child, they can build their relationship with them by showing them love, appreciation, and the importance of reading. This helps children to develop trust and self-esteem as they feel cared for and loved by caregivers. Often when children's needs are not being met through time spent with their parents or caregivers, these functions can improve with more time spent together.

Reading aloud can benefit children of all ages, from infants to older children. It can also be an enjoyable activity for caregivers and children and can be incorporated into daily routines, such as bedtime or nap time. In addition to the benefits for children, reading aloud can also benefit caregivers, as it can provide a break from screens and technology and promote relaxation and stress relief.

Choosing age-appropriate books

There is no "right" or "wrong" age for children to begin reading. Although young children may learn essential skills from vocal instruction, research suggests that reading to children improves their ability to learn. Educators and speech pathologists may recommend that young children read aloud because it helps them acquire these skills. Books should be chosen based on interest, vocabulary level, and appropriateness for the child's developmental stage.

When choosing books for a child, it is essential to consider each book's vocabulary, subject, and illustrations. Each book should be selected based on its content, with close attention to vocabulary and issues. When reading aloud, it is essential to use developmentally appropriate and exciting words for the child. If a child is struggling with sounding out words, it may be beneficial to read with a limited number of words first and have them repeat back what they have heard.

Books can be chosen based on the subject that interests the child. Reading about familiar topics such as family pets and toys or places in their community can help keep children interested in reading.

Choosing age-appropriate books is essential for promoting children's literacy and language development. Here are some tips for selecting books that are appropriate for your child's age:

Consider your child's reading level

Choose books that match your child's reading level. If your child is starting to read, look for books with simple words and short sentences, while more advanced readers may be able to handle longer books with more complex vocabulary and themes.

Look for books with consistent illustrations and characters. It won't mean anything to the child if you don't know a word's definition. By providing your child with recognizable characters in a familiar setting, children are more likely to develop confidence in their reading abilities and remember what they read.

Choose books that have a consistent theme, setting, or plot. For example, if your child loves animals, then choose books that feature animals or have animal characters. If you are looking for books about science or math—or find the products about these topics interesting—then look for books that make these topics fun for your child by providing vivid illustrations that illustrate concepts easily.

Look for books with age-appropriate themes

Choose books with themes and topics appropriate for your child's age and developmental stage. For example, books about friendship and emotions may be more suitable for young children. In contrast, books about more complex issues like identity and social justice may be more appropriate for older children.

Create an environment that supports reading

Reading aloud can be fun and worthwhile for both children and adults. To read aloud, you need to have a quiet environment that is free of distractions. This could mean creating a reading nook or choosing a time when your child is less busy, like after dinner or nap time. It's helpful to maintain the same routine so that your child can get into the habit of looking forward to reading time.

For caregivers and parents, reading aloud with children is essential to nurturing positive development in their language and literacy skills. Reading aloud helps them learn about the world and develop language skills - both are essential for children's academic success.

Pay attention to the illustrations

Children's books often have just as essential illustrations as the words themselves. Look for illustrations that are colorful, engaging, and match the tone of the story. Children should be encouraged to highlight objects in the images and describe what they see. Also, encourage your child to draw pictures and connect the pictures with words.

Keep engaging in positive activities

Investing time in reading is essential to fostering children's language development, literacy skills, and love of learning. Changing up the activity by choosing different books or ways to read can help make reading more fun and exciting for you and your child.

Consider your child's interests

Choose books that match your child's interests and hobbies. For example, if your child is interested in dinosaurs, look for books about dinosaurs. If your child loves animals, look for books about animals. If your child loves to read, find books similar to those they already like.

It is also important to note that reading aloud should not cause stress or anxiety in children. As parents or caregivers, we need to find enjoyment and fun in reading aloud with children and enjoy the rich experience it brings us.

Check reviews and recommendations

Look for recommendations from trusted sources, such as librarians, teachers, or parenting websites. You can also check online reviews to understand what other parents and children have enjoyed.

Choosing age-appropriate books can help children develop a love of reading and promote their literacy and language development. By selecting books appropriate for your child's age, interests, and reading level, you can help foster a lifelong love of reading and learning.

There are many benefits to reading aloud to children, including language development. Reading aloud helps children learn about language and the world around them. Raising a child's vocabulary is a lifelong commitment, and reading aloud is one of the best ways to start. It can also improve performance in other academic subjects and their self-confidence and social skills.

Reading aloud allows caregivers and parents to bond with their children, providing a more positive parent-child relationship. When interacting with a caregiver, infants begin to feel more positive toward that person and establish an early connection that promotes attachment and bonding.

Tips for engaging storytelling

Storytelling is a great way to explore the world of literature, history, and all forms of culture. Engaging young children with engaging stories of interest and adventure can be a relaxing experience.

Storytelling is a great way to promote children's language and literacy development, as well as their imagination and creativity. Here are some tips for engaging storytelling:

Use expressive language

Use expressive and engaging language to help bring the story to life. Vary your tone of voice, use different accents and characters, and emphasize keywords and phrases.

Use distinguishing voices

It can help children distinguish different characters and track who is who. It also conveys a lot of details in a short amount of time.

Use character voices

To help children learn about personalities and develop empathy, you can use different voices for different characters to reflect these differences. For example, if a character is mean, you can use an angry or gruff voice; if the character is happy and bubbly, you can use a light, high-pitched voice.

Look at pictures and make up your own story

Please encourage your child to look at the pictures while narrating the story, then encourage them to make up their own story based on what they see in the pictures.

Incorporate gestures and facial expressions

Use gestures and facial expressions to help illustrate the story and convey emotions. For example, use hand gestures to show the size of a character or the movement of an object, or use facial expressions to show surprise or excitement.

Use props and visuals

Props and visuals can help make the story more engaging and memorable. For example, use a puppet or stuffed animal to represent a character or use pictures or illustrations to show critical scenes or characters.

Encourage participation

Encourage children to participate in the story by asking questions, making predictions, or even acting out parts of the story. This can help keep children engaged and promote their comprehension and understanding.

Choose age-appropriate stories

Choose stories that are appropriate for your child's age and developmental stage. Younger children may enjoy simple plots and repetitive language, while older children prefer more complex stories with multiple characters and themes.

Practice and prepare

Practice telling the story before you share it with your child. This can help you feel more confident and comfortable and allow you to focus on engaging storytelling techniques.

Using these tips, you can help make storytelling a fun and engaging activity that promotes children's language and literacy development, imagination and creativity, and overall enjoyment of stories.

Chapter 9. Week 4 - Singing and Music

Singing is a great way to get toddlers to talk. Singing and music can be beneficial for speech development in children. Here are some ways in which music can promote speech and language development:

Rhythm and timing: Music has a predictable rhythm and timing that can help children develop their sense of rhythm and timing. This can be beneficial for speech development, as it can help children learn to pace their speech and use appropriate timing when speaking.

Vocabulary development: Singing and music can expose children to new words and vocabulary, enhancing their language development and communication skills. Songs often use repetition and rhyme, which can help children remember new terms and concepts.

Pronunciation and articulation: Singing and music can help children practice pronunciation and articulation as they learn to match the rhythm and timing of the song with the sounds they produce. This can be especially helpful for children with difficulty with speech sounds or articulation.

Memory and recall: Music can be a powerful tool for memory and recall, which can help children remember new words and phrases more easily.

Engagement and motivation: Singing and music can be fun activities that motivate children to participate and practice their speech and language skills.

Choosing age-appropriate songs and activities is essential when singing and using music to promote speech development. For example, younger children may enjoy simple songs with repetitive language, while older children may enjoy more complex songs with multiple verses and choruses. Creating a positive and supportive environment where children feel comfortable and encouraged to participate and practice their speech and language skills is also essential.

The Role of Music in language development

Music can be a powerful tool in the language development of young children. It can provide a fun and engaging activity for children and promote language development in several ways.

Music and rhythm

Music and rhythms can be vital tools for language development. Music has a natural rhythm, which can help children develop their sense of rhythm, which will help them when speaking or singing. Rhythm may also influence the words they choose when speaking or singing. Rhyming songs can help children learn new words, as they associate the new term with the song and sing it more often. Teaching music improves reading skills in young children at risk of reading failure. Infants develop language skills more quickly when parents play music and sing to their children.

Music and Memory

Music can be a powerful tool for memory, which can help children learn new vocabulary or concepts that they cannot yet express in words. Songs often have melodies and rhythms that are easy for children to remember, which can help them recall the information in the song more easily. Singing songs may also help children remember words and phrases longer than if they repeat them verbally.

Music and motivation

Singing songs together as a family or group can be fun to motivate children to practice their speaking skills. They will want to participate in the activity and may feel motivated to use their words and speak while they sing.

Choosing the right song is essential when choosing music or singing activities for language development. Younger children may enjoy songs with simple vocabulary, straightforward rhythms, and a predictable structure. Older children may want more complex songs with more verses and choruses to practice fluency as they sing.

The relationship between music and language is vital in children. Learning music can help children develop their sense of rhythm, which will help them when speaking or singing. As children learn to play an instrument or sing in a choir, they can develop their vocabulary by learning new words and phrases. Music can be a powerful tool for memory, so children may be able to absorb more information when singing songs rather than just reciting the information verbally.

Music therapy is considered an effective treatment for sound speech disorders. Children who participate in music classes or musical activities tend to have better speech development than those who do not. Singing songs can help children practice pronunciation and articulation, which benefits those with speech sound disorders. When singing to a child with a sound speech disorder, it is important to use songs focusing on vowels, not consonants. Vowels are more stable, and children with speech sound disorders can learn to control their sounds better using vowels.

Music used in therapy is also effective with children who have autism. Music can help calm the child and reduce stress, essential for communication development. Music therapy can also be used as a reward for positive communication or behavior.

Music used in therapy may also be beneficial in treating children with apraxia of speech (AOS). Children with AOS benefit from music therapy because it improves auditory processing, allowing them to process spoken language more accurately.

Music can play an essential role in language development in children.

Here are some ways that music can support language development:

Exposure to new words and sounds: Songs and music can expose children to new words, phrases, and sounds they might not hear in everyday speech. This can help expand their vocabulary and improve their ability to recognize and differentiate between different sounds.

Repetition and memorization: Many songs have repetitive lyrics and melodies, which can help children learn and memorize new words and phrases more easily. This can also help reinforce their understanding of grammatical structures and sentence patterns.

Rhythm and timing: Music has a natural rhythm and timing, which can help children develop their sense of rhythm and timing, which is vital for language development. This can help them learn to recognize and produce the rhythms and patterns of spoken language.

Emotional engagement: Music can be a powerful emotional tool that can engage children and help them connect with the words and messages in a song. This emotional engagement can help reinforce their understanding and retention of language.

Multimodal learning: Music engages multiple senses, including hearing, movement, and sometimes sight, which can help support children's learning and memory. For example, clapping or dancing along with a song can help reinforce the rhythm and timing of the lyrics.

Overall, music can be a fun and engaging way to support language development in children. Parents and caregivers can incorporate music and singing into their daily routines and choose age-appropriate songs that expose children to new vocabulary and language patterns.

Singing nursery rhymes and songs

Sing your baby a song because it's the way, it's the way to his heart. Singing nursery rhymes and songs to your child can have several positive impacts on his language development:

Improving language skills: Singing simple rhymes and songs with your baby can help him develop better language skills. Repeating words and phrases in nursery rhymes can reinforce his understanding of new vocabulary. Repeating sing-along songs during playtime can also help teach him new words as he learns them while participating in the activity.

Developing rhythm and timing: Singing nursery rhymes with your baby can help you build your child's ability to produce the rhythm and timing of spoken language. This can help reinforce his ability to perceive and produce the sounds of words.

Encouraging movement: Singing, swaying, and clapping along with a song can help teach your child how to move as he learns the lyrics and rhythms of spoken language. This helps support his motor skills and hand-eye coordination, essential for communication development.

Improving hearing: Singing nursery rhymes and songs with your baby can help your child's hearing, which is essential for early language development. Hearing sounds will help her identify them in spoken language and be better able to imitate them once she begins to speak.

Preventing speech disorders: Singing nursery rhymes and songs with your baby can help avoid speech disorders. Children who sing nursery rhymes while still in the womb can develop better language.

Singing nursery rhymes and songs early in life is beneficial for the child's speech and language development, as it can help him understand new words and phrases as he grows older.

Singing songs during playtime with your child will develop his motor skills, vocabulary, motor planning skills, hand-eye coordination, vocal pitch, rhythm, and functional speech organ systems.

When children begin to talk, they may make up their first words from nursery rhymes or songs they know from daycare or family members. Allowing them to say the word how they would sing it is essential. For example, a child may say "caca" instead of "cat." If a child uses a song as part of their first words, it is good to continue using it when you tell him or again later.

Vocabulary development: Nursery rhymes and songs often use simple, repetitive language that can help children learn new words and phrases.

Phonemic awareness: Nursery rhymes and songs often have rhyming words and patterns, which can help children develop their phonemic awareness and understanding of how words sound.

Memory and recall: Nursery rhymes and songs are often memorable and easy to remember, which can help children with memory and recall.

Social and emotional development: Singing and sharing nursery rhymes and songs with others can be a fun and engaging social activity that promotes bonding and emotional expression.

Cultural literacy: Nursery rhymes and songs often reflect cultural traditions and values and can help children develop an understanding and appreciation for their cultural heritage and other cultures.

When singing nursery rhymes and songs with children, choosing age-appropriate songs and activities is essential. Younger children may enjoy simple, repetitive songs with catchy tunes and hand gestures, while older children may enjoy more complex songs with multiple verses and choruses. Parents and caregivers can also use nursery rhymes and songs to engage children in conversation, asking them questions about the lyrics and encouraging them to share their ideas and experiences. Singing nursery rhymes and songs can be a fun and effective way to support children's language development while promoting social and emotional growth.

Encouraging movement and dance

Encourage movement and dance with your child because it's the way, it's the way to his heart. Movement can help develop children's language skills, social-emotional development, motor skills, and gross motor skills. The impact of dancing on motor development is well documented in studies, so it is essential to include movement and dance in your daily routines with your child.

Encouraging movement and dance can benefit children's overall development and language skills. Here are some ways that movement and dance can support language development:

Motor skills development

Dancing and moving to music can help children develop their gross and fine motor skills, supporting their ability to coordinate and control their movements in speaking and other language-related activities.

Encouraging expressive communication

Engaging with your child through movement can encourage him to use expressive communication to meet his needs, express his emotions and connect with others. This will help him communicate his wants and needs effectively as he ages.

Encouraging social connection through playtime

Children need opportunities to engage socially with their parents or caregivers. You can encourage social connection through playtime activities, such as singing and listening to music with your child.

Social development

Social connection is essential for the child's development and their relationships with caregivers. Children who are more socially connected will have happier, healthier lives.

Body awareness

Movement and dance can help children develop a greater awareness of their bodies and how they move, which can support their ability to understand and use spatial language (e.g., "up," "down," "over," "under").

Rhythm and timing

Dance and movement involve a sense of rhythm and timing similar to spoken language's rhythms and patterns. Practicing rhythm and timing through dance and movement can help children develop their ability to recognize and produce the rhythms and patterns of language.

Vocabulary development

Dance and movement can expose children to new words and phrases related to movement and physical activity. For example, they may learn words like "jump," "spin," "twirl," "stretch," and "balance."

Sensory stimulation

Dance and movement can provide children with sensory stimuli supporting language development. For example, touch and movement help children learn about the words and phrases related to sensation, such as "hot," "cold," "soft," or "rough."

Attention and focus

Movement and dance can help improve children's attention and focus, supporting their ability to listen and communicate effectively.

Parents and caregivers can incorporate music and movement into their daily routines to encourage movement and dance in children. This can include activities like dancing to music, playing games that involve movement (e.g., "Simon Says"), and participating in physical activities like yoga or sports. Creating a positive and supportive environment where children feel comfortable and encouraged to participate and practice their language and movement skills is essential.

Chapter 10. Week 5 - Playtime and Language

Playtime and language refer to the idea that play is crucial to children's language development. Play is a natural way for children to learn and practice new skills, and language development is no exception. During playtime, children can practice communication skills such as listening, speaking, and social interaction.

Playtime can take many forms, from imaginative play to outdoor activities, and can be facilitated by parents, caregivers, or peers. Playtime provides opportunities for children to engage in language-rich activities that support their vocabulary, grammar, and communication skills. For example, parents and caregivers can play pretend with children, read books together, or play language-based games to encourage language development.

Playtime allows children to explore their world, interact with others, and develop social skills. Playing with others teaches children how to take turns, cooperate, and negotiate, all essential communication skills. Playtime and language go hand in hand as play provides an excellent opportunity for children to learn and practice their language skills naturally and enjoyably.

Here are some ways playtime can support language development:

Imaginative play: Imaginative play, such as pretend play or role-playing, can help children practice their language skills by using their imagination and creating scenarios that require communication and social interaction.

Games: Playing games that involve turn-taking, following rules, and using language to communicate can help children develop their language and social skills.

Storytelling: Reading books or telling stories during playtime can help children develop their listening and comprehension skills, as well as their vocabulary and understanding of narrative structure.

Art activities: Art activities, such as drawing or painting, can provide opportunities for children to express themselves verbally and visually, as well as practice describing their artwork and discussing their ideas.

Outdoor play: Outdoor play allows children to explore the natural world, practice physical coordination, and interact socially with peers.

Following the child's lead and interests is essential when engaging in playtime activities to support language development. Parents and caregivers can observe the child's play and provide supportive language input, such as labeling objects or actions, asking open-ended questions, and giving feedback and praise. Additionally, providing various play materials and activities can help keep playtime engaging and stimulating for the child.

Play-based language activities

Play-based language activities refer to using play to develop and practice language skills in children. These activities involve using play to encourage children to communicate, interact, and practice language skills naturally and enjoyably.

Play-based language activities can include a wide range of activities, such as pretend play, building and construction, art activities, language-based games, and outdoor play. These activities help children develop their vocabulary, grammar, communication, and social skills.

For example, during pretend play, children can use language to communicate and interact with others while taking on different roles and scenarios. Building and construction activities can provide opportunities for children to describe what they are building, ask for materials or help from others, and engage in imaginative play scenarios. Art activities can allow children to describe their artwork, talk about the colors or shapes they are using, and engage in creative storytelling based on their artwork. Language-based games can help children practice their listening and speaking skills while having fun, and outdoor play can provide opportunities for children to engage in physical activities while practicing their language skills.

Play-based language activities are a fun and effective way for children to develop and practice their language skills naturally and enjoyably. Parents and caregivers can support these activities by providing various play materials and opportunities, asking open-ended questions, and providing feedback and praise.

Many play-based activities can be used to support language development. Here are some examples:

Pretend and role-playing games: Pretend and role-playing games allow children to practice using language in a fun and playful way, such as playing house, having "tea parties," or playing doctor.

Imaginative stories: Parents and caregivers can read books or tell stories incorporating familiar terms and use descriptive language to encourage children to ask questions, label objects, name characters, or retell the story.

Play dough: Using play dough for pretend activities or making cookies with play dough can provide opportunities for children to describe their creations and ask questions about cooking or baking.

Puppets and dolls: Puppets or dolls can provide opportunities for children to act out stories, use descriptive language to describe their actions, and practice asking others for things.

Writing: When writing letters, making lists, or drawing pictures to accompany stories, children can practice their spelling and descriptive language skills.

Building and construction: Building with blocks or out of paper can be a fun way for children to let their imaginations run wild and practice describing their actions.

Art activities allow children to express themselves artistically while practicing their literacy skills. For example, children can use colored pencils to express their feelings about a situation, make a collage of favorite animals, create a picture telling their day's story, or illustrate a favorite book.

Outdoor play: Playing in the yard allows children to practice running and jumping while using language to communicate with others.

Following the child's lead and interests is essential when engaging in play-based language activities to support language development. Parents and caregivers can observe the child's play and provide supportive language input, such as labeling objects or actions, asking open-ended questions, and giving feedback and praise. Additionally, providing various play materials and opportunities for play can keep play-based language activities fun and engaging for the child.

Play is integral to helping children develop their language skills, but it's important to remember that playing with your child isn't the only way to support language development. Parents and caregivers can also practice simple activities throughout their day that can help develop and support language skills at home, such as reading stories, talking with their child, having conversations, singing songs or playing music together, playing games, or participating in outdoor activities.

Pretend play scenarios

Pretend play scenarios are imaginary situations that children create and act out using their imagination and creativity. In pretend play, children take on different roles, such as a doctor, a teacher, a firefighter, or a superhero, and engage in play scenarios that mimic real-life situations.

For example, a child might pretend to be a chef and use their toy kitchen for cooking imaginary meals, or they might pretend to be a doctor and give check-ups to their stuffed animals. Pretend play scenarios allow children to practice and develop their language skills by communicating and interacting with others in different roles and situations.

Pretend play scenarios also allow children to develop social and emotional skills by exploring different perspectives, practicing empathy, and learning to negotiate and cooperate. Children can develop problem-solving and critical thinking skills through pretend play by creating creative solutions to imaginary problems and challenges.

Pretend play scenarios can be supported and encouraged by providing children with age-appropriate toys and props that allow them to imagine and create different scenarios. Parents and caregivers can also participate in pretend play scenarios with their children, strengthening parent-child relationships and providing opportunities for children to learn from adult role models.

Pretend play scenarios can involve any number of roles, settings, or activities and are often inspired by real-life experiences, stories, or media.

Examples of pretend play scenarios might include:

Playing house: children might take on roles such as mother, father, or child and use toys or props to act out everyday activities like cooking, cleaning, or caring for a baby doll.

Dress-up: children might put on costumes or use props to become characters from books, movies, or their imagination and act out scenes or stories.

Superhero play: children might pretend to have superpowers and engage in make-believe battles or missions to save the day.

Restaurant play: children might create menus, take orders, and prepare imaginary meals for their customers.

Animal play: children might take on the roles of different animals, exploring their habitats, behaviors, and interactions with other animals.

Inventing: children might be creative in pretend play scenarios, such as creating new clothes for dolls or new games for toys.

Parents and caregivers can encourage the development of pretend-to-play through modeling. For example, while playing house, parents and caregivers can show their children how to play different roles, take on different perspectives, solve problems together, or share responsibilities. Parents and caregivers can also create opportunities for children by providing them with toys and props that might spark their imaginations.

Parents and caregivers should also ensure children have opportunities to engage in free play, which is when children use their imagination with minimal adult intervention. Free play allows children to explore their interests independently and learn new skills through experimentation. Adults often facilitate play, but it is essential to remember that children learn best when they can explore their interests and engage in pretend play scenarios independently.

Pretend play scenarios offer numerous benefits for children's development, including opportunities for creativity, imagination, and social and language skills. By taking on different roles and engaging in make-believe scenarios, children can explore different perspectives, learn to cooperate and negotiate with others, and develop empathy and understanding for others. Pretend play scenarios can also help children develop problem-solving and critical thinking skills as they develop creative solutions to imaginary problems and challenges.

Parents and caregivers can support children's pretend play scenarios by providing them with age-appropriate toys, costumes, and props and creating a safe and supportive environment to explore their imagination and creativity. Parents can also participate in pretend play scenarios with their children, strengthening parent-child relationships and providing opportunities for children to learn from adult role models.

Interactive games and activities

Interactive games and activities are pretended scenarios that allow children to practice the social and language skills they have learned. These play acts are inspired by the idea that children talk and interact with one another differently when playing together versus when playing alone.

Interactive games and activities are play-based experiences that promote children's language development and social interaction. These activities involve active participation and engagement from children and can be designed for individual or group play.

Examples of interactive games and activities include:

Board games: Board games are an excellent way to promote social interaction and language development. Games such as Chutes and Ladders, Candy Land, or Sorry! It can help children learn to take turns, follow the rules, and communicate with others.

Card games: Card games like Go Fish, Old Maid, or Uno can help children develop language and social skills by practicing communication, turn-taking, and negotiation.

Storytelling games: Games encouraging storytelling, such as "Once Upon a Time" or "Story Cubes," can help children develop their imagination, creativity, and language skills.

Interactive apps and online games: Interactive apps and online games can be an engaging way to promote language development in children. Games like "Endless Alphabet" or "ABCmouse" can help children learn new words and practice letter recognition and phonics skills.

Building and construction sets: Building and construction sets such as Lego or Duplo can help children develop fine motor skills and spatial awareness while promoting language development through collaborative play and problem-solving.

Role-playing: children might take on different roles, such as puppet master, chef, or teacher, and use their imagination to act out game scenarios like pretending to cook dinner or teach a lesson.

Cooperation games: children might engage in pretend play scenarios based on real-life situations where they learn how to collaborate as a group or negotiate as individuals.

Role-reversal games: children might pretend to take on different roles or perspectives other than their own, such as pretending to be a baby so they can be rocked or fed by their parent or caregiver.

Technology-based games: children might pretend to use imaginary gadgets like phones and computers when playing with toys.

Instructive games: children pretend to be giving lessons using flashcards and other props.

Helping games: where children engage in pretend play scenarios based on real-life experiences where they learn to be helpful and take care of others.

Physical games: where children engage in pretend play scenarios inspired by physical activities such as roller skating, dancing, or running.

Interactive games can help children develop language skills by speaking and listening to one another, using turn-taking cues, and following rules. These games also allow children to explore ideas out loud with peers or adults, which helps them practice problem-solving skills when one person says something the other does not understand. Interactive games can also help children learn to cooperate with others and be more tolerant toward those who have different opinions or reactions to a given situation.

Interactive games also involve more than one child, so they can help children practice their social skills with peers. Parents and caregivers can model verbal interactions for children by assisting them in practicing the language that can be used during pretend play scenarios. For example, parents and caregivers can model how children might ask a peer for a toy, such as "Can I have the truck?" or "Can you give me that toy?"

Parents and caregivers should avoid using real-life interactions when playing interactive games with their children. Playing out real-life interactions may confuse children just learning how to interact with others, mainly if these interactions occur during an outburst or end in conflict or frustration. Suppose children are learning about pretend play scenarios and their interactions with others. Parents and caregivers should set up the scenario and let children figure out the rules independently.

Interactive games and activities can be adapted to suit the age and interests of the child. They can be a fun and effective way to support language development and social interaction. Parents and caregivers can participate in these activities with their children to promote family bonding and create a positive and supportive learning environment.

Chapter 11. Week 6 - Reinforcing Progress and Moving Forward

Reinforcing progress and moving forward means recognizing and celebrating a child's milestones and achievements in their language development while setting new goals and supporting their growth.

Positive reinforcement and praise are essential when a child progresses in language development. This can be done through verbal affirmation, such as saying "good job" or "well done," or through tangible rewards, such as stickers or small treats.

However, it's also essential to challenge the child and set new goals to encourage continued growth. This can involve introducing new vocabulary and more complex language concepts or setting goals for improving pronunciation or grammar.

Parents and caregivers can also involve the child in setting goals and monitoring their progress. This can help the child take ownership of their language development and feel accomplished when they meet their goals.

Reinforcing progress and moving forward is about creating a positive and supportive learning environment that encourages children to continue developing their language skills and reaching their full potential.

Assessing progress

Assessing progress means evaluating the child's language skills. Assessing progress in language development is essential in ensuring that a child is meeting age-appropriate milestones and progressing towards their language goals. There are several ways that progress can be assessed, including:

Observing the child's spontaneous use of language and any similarities or differences between their speech and the speech of others. Observe how the child responds when language is used with them, such as how they react when you speak to or read to them and how they interact with others in conversation.

What's important is that you find out what the child knows and can do, then set goals for encouraging further progress.

This involves observing and documenting what a child does (or does not) know about grammar, vocabulary, sound production, and communication skills. Given children develop at different rates, it's also essential to determine what a typical development might look like for a particular age range or stage.

Assessment can be done in several ways, such as interviewing the child to gain insight into their language development, observing them and recording what they do, or assessing them on a formal test (such as one from SACCO). It's also essential to set and monitor goals for the child's language development so that you can evaluate their progress.

Setting goals

Setting goals means deciding on clear and achievable targets for the child to work towards. Setting goals involves reviewing what you know about their progress - such as their strengths, difficulties, and learning styles - then setting targets based on these assessments.

Setting goals is often done by talking with the parent, caregiver, or therapist familiar with the child. These professionals will have already put in place plans for the child's language development, so they should be able to clearly describe the child's current stage and rate of language development.

You can also base your goals on your observations of the child and their language test results. For example, suppose you notice they have difficulty using pronouns correctly and are often unsure when to use them. In that case, you might decide that their goals should include using pronouns more often in conversation. This would mean trying to get them to talk about particular topics at the start of a conversation so that they can learn more about those topics by asking questions.

You could also ask the parents or caregivers to complete a language questionnaire and use the results to set goals.

Setting goals for your child is integral to helping them meet their full potential in language development.

Using developmental checklists: Developmental checklists are lists of language milestones and behaviors a child is expected to reach at a certain age. These checklists can assess a child's progress and identify areas needing additional support.

Consulting with a speech-language pathologist: A speech-language pathologist (SLP) specializes in diagnosing and treating language and communication disorders. An SLP can perform formal assessments to evaluate a child's language abilities and identify any areas of concern.

Using standardized assessments: Standardized assessments are formal tests used to evaluate a child's language abilities. These assessments can provide detailed information about a child's language strengths and weaknesses and can help guide interventions and treatment plans.

Assessing progress in language development is an ongoing process and should be done regularly to ensure that the child is progressing and receiving appropriate support. By identifying areas of concern and addressing them early on, parents and caregivers can help ensure that the child reaches their full language potential

Overcoming challenges

Language development is a continuous process. Just like with other areas of development, there are times when the child's language skills may not seem to be as advanced as they should be. This is also true in the context of language development and learning disorders.

All children have challenges and setbacks throughout their language development, and there are many strategies that parents can use to address these issues and ensure that they keep moving forward.

Overcoming challenges in language development can be a complex and ongoing process. Here are some strategies that can be helpful for parents and caregivers:

Seek professional help: If you suspect your child may be experiencing challenges in their language development, it's essential to seek professional help from a speech-language pathologist (SLP) or another qualified professional. These professionals can evaluate your child's language abilities and guide interventions and treatment plans.

Provide a supportive environment: A supportive and nurturing environment can help children feel more comfortable and confident in practicing their language skills. This can involve giving them plenty of opportunities to practice, providing positive feedback and encouragement, and creating a safe space to express themselves without fear of judgment.

Use various teaching strategies: Children learn in different ways, so it's essential to use multiple teaching strategies to support their language development. This can involve using visual aids, such as pictures or videos, incorporating hands-on activities, and using repetition and reinforcement to help solidify new concepts.

Be patient and persistent: Language development can be slow and gradual, and progress may not be immediately noticeable. It's essential to be patient and persistent and to celebrate even small victories along the way.

Incorporate language practice into everyday activities: Incorporating language practice into daily activities can help children see the practical value of language skills and make language learning feel more natural and enjoyable. This can involve singing songs, playing games, and conversing during daily routines like mealtime or bath time.

Overcoming challenges in language development requires a collaborative effort between parents, caregivers, and qualified professionals. Children can overcome challenges and reach their full language potential by working together and providing consistent support.

Continuing support beyond the 6-week plan

The 6-week plan is designed to help parents and caregivers solidify their child's language development foundations. By following the steps outlined in this program, parents and caregivers can provide the support their child needs to develop an early love for language, which will help them reach their full potential.

Supporting beyond a 6-week plan ensures children's language development progress. Here are some strategies for providing ongoing support:

Set new goals: Once the initial 6-week plan is complete, it's essential to set new goals to work towards. This can involve identifying new skills to work on or building upon the progress already made.

Regular check-ins with a speech-language pathologist or other qualified professionals can help ensure that children continue progressing and receive the support they need.

Continue to use language-rich activities: Incorporating language-rich activities into everyday routines and exercises can help children continue to practice and improve their language skills. This can involve reading books, singing songs, and playing pretend.

Provide positive feedback: Continued positive feedback and encouragement can help children feel confident and motivated to continue practicing their language skills.

Adjust interventions as needed: As children's language skills continue to develop, it may be necessary to adjust interventions and strategies to meet their changing needs.

By providing ongoing support and making adjustments as needed, children can continue to make progress in their language development and reach their full potential.

Chapter 12. Tips for Maintaining Progress and Addressing Setbacks

Addressing setbacks is vital because progress is not linear, and the road has inevitable bumps. If your child has slowed their speech development, please don't despair! There may be something going on that you're unaware of that's causing this delay. You'll need to determine the cause of the setback and then address that problem. You may have gotten frustrated with your child and taken a break from speech work, leading to a longer-than-expected delay in progress. Not only that but you could be easily distracted by daily activities, which makes it hard to spend time practicing speech every day. Or perhaps you've been away on vacation or other trips, which can also slow progress.

Compile a list of possible causes for your child's setback, then systematically rule out each one, so you can pinpoint the real culprit. Once this is accomplished, you can make any necessary adjustments early so your child doesn't fall too far behind.

Encouraging ongoing language development

Encouraging ongoing language development in children can help them progress and build upon their skills over time. Here are some strategies for encouraging ongoing language development:

Engage in regular conversations: Regularly engaging children in conversations can help them practice their language skills and develop their ability to express themselves.

Read together: Reading books together can help children develop their vocabulary, comprehension, and literacy skills. It's also an excellent opportunity to engage children in conversation and discuss the story.

Play games that involve language: Games that involve language, such as word games or storytelling games, can help children practice their language skills in a fun and engaging way.

Encourage writing and drawing: Encouraging children to write and draw can help them develop their literacy skills and express themselves through written language.

Provide a language-rich environment: Providing a language-rich environment that includes opportunities for listening, speaking, reading, and writing can help children continue to develop their language skills.

By incorporating these strategies into everyday routines and activities, parents and caregivers can help support ongoing language development in children and set them up for success in the future.

Don't stop working on speech just because your child is talking! It's easy to assume that all speech intervention is over once a child starts talking, but this is false. If possible, you should be working on speech until your child is three. Don't stop simply because you can understand what they're saying. Don't stop simply because they start putting words together without prompting. Keep going until you hear sentences with a grammatical structure indicating real language development.

This means you may need to be creative with your speech activities. If your child talks more, they may feel less motivated to practice speech. So, find new and fun ways to reinforce the type of speech work you do daily. For example, instead of sorting pictures only when prompted by your child, please talk about the pictures as you sort them. Maybe your child will start joining in with a word or two now and again on his own. Remember that these "word" attempts are just sounds or syllables, so reinforce these by responding with a word or phrase when he does this.

Remember, this is still significant work! Speech delays and disorders have been linked to many other problems, including ADHD, Autism, learning disabilities, and more. So please don't stop doing progress-monitoring activities once your child talks alone.

It's easy to be motivated to work with your child when they progress slowly. After all, short-term gains and confidence boosts from working on speech every day are immediate and rewarding for parents. But once your child starts talking, it can be difficult for parents to continue working on speech as diligently as before.

Handling setbacks and plateaus

Handling setbacks and plateaus is essential to maintaining your child's speech development over the long term. Setbacks and plateaus can be frustrating, but they are a normal part of the language development process. Here are some strategies for handling setbacks and plateaus:

Maintain your schedule: Taking a break from everyday speech work can be very tempting once your child starts talking alone. But it would be best to continue working on speech daily to keep moving forward. Don't stop unless you're going through a period where you just aren't able to work on speech as frequently as before, such as if you have a newborn at home or if your child is having trouble sleeping and taking short naps during the day because they aren't sleeping through the night yet.

Take a break: If you feel your child is getting stuck during speech work because they are bored, lack attention, or seem uninterested, then it may be time to take a short break from working on a speech for a few days and then resume again. Taking short breaks may help push your child through plateau periods.

Resume working on a regular schedule: If you are hitting plateaus, try resuming working on speech every day at the same time rather than setting up separate appointments with your child. This can help you maintain consistency and continuity in the type of language work you are doing.

Learn from your child: If you find that you and your child aren't progressing on a particular speech goal, then it may be time to evaluate the goals you are working on. Take a step back and look at what type of goals are appropriate for your child's age and skill level. You can also review which goals have been mastered by looking at the charts or data you've been keeping.

Stay positive: A positive attitude can help children stay motivated and focused on their goals. Encourage children to keep trying and remind them of their progress so far.

Practice regularly: Consistent practice is critical to making progress in language development. Encourage children to practice their language skills regularly, even if progress seems slow.

Celebrate small victories: Celebrating small victories along the way can help children stay motivated and engaged in the language development process.

Seek support: Don't hesitate to seek support from a speech-language pathologist or other qualified professionals if progress has stalled or you feel overwhelmed.

Remember that every child is unique and progresses at their own pace. With patience, persistence, and the proper support, children can overcome setbacks and plateaus and progress in their language development.

Once you've identified where your child is getting stuck, think about how to present the material in a way that works better with their skills. Maybe your child needs more practice in the receptive language area to better understand their role during therapy sessions. Or perhaps your child's speech is so unclear that you need to work on helping him learn to be more specific with his descriptions of objects and activities.

Seeking additional support when needed

Seeking additional support can be beneficial for children experiencing language development difficulties. Here are some professionals who may be able to provide support:

Speech-language pathologist: A speech-language pathologist is a trained professional who can assess and treat speech and language disorders. They can work with children and their families to develop individualized treatment plans for specific needs.

Pediatrician: A pediatrician can provide general guidance on child development and refer families to specialists. They may also be able to identify red flags or warning signs for language delays.

Early intervention program: Early intervention programs provide services to children with developmental delays or disabilities, including speech and language delays. These programs may be provided through the local school district or community-based organizations.

Education Specialist: An education specialist can guide educational strategies and accommodations to support language development in children struggling in school.

Psychologist: A psychologist can support children experiencing emotional or behavioral challenges that may impact their language development.

Remember that seeking support is a sign of strength, and it can be helpful for both the child and the family. By working with professionals specializing in language development, families can get the support they need to help their child progress and reach their full potential.

As with any development area, getting additional support when necessary, can be beneficial. It can be challenging to work through a child's speech delays or disorders without the help of a professional. That's why finding a speech-language pathologist trained in working with children with speech delays and disorders is essential.

Finding a qualified speech-language pathologist may not always be as difficult as you think. You might ask for recommendations from friends and family members who know someone who is an expert in working with young children with language disorders. Think about local preschools, daycare centers, and school districts, too.

If you don't find support from other speech-language pathologists, you may consider getting your child referred to a tertiary service provider. Tertiary providers provide services at the primary and secondary levels of speech-language pathology and the tertiary level. They also provide services for families of individuals with language disorders.

When hiring a speech or educational therapist, consider their experience treating young children with language disorders. Check references and credentials before making an appointment with a potential provider.

Conclusion

You should take action if your child is not speaking by age 3. It might be tempting to wait it out or hope your child will eventually catch up, but the reality is that we have a limited window of time in which to foster communication and language skills. The early stages are critical for learning a language, so if they're not getting it now, they may never experience what makes communication so incredibly rewarding.

It's hard to say whether your toddler will eventually speak once he gets older and goes through more experiences with people around him. Ultimately, you'll just have to wait and see this over time. But the reality is that if your child doesn't speak, Your Child's Speech and Language Development won't progress as much.

I suggest this: don't wait too long to start working on speech and language. Your toddler might be too little to tell you when he needs some help, but you must get started in the grand scheme of things. The earlier you start, the more quickly your child will catch up.

If your child is already speaking, then there are still a few things you can do to help his skills grow and develop into a mature adult-like speech pattern sooner rather than later.

The first step to helping your toddler learn how to talk is identifying his "words". We have identified four words as the most common: milk, cup, juice box, and fork. If you ask him these words, he will try to say them back to you (with a bit of practice – sometimes, he might try using food instead of utensils). It is crucial for us parents not to confuse our child with more complicated words such as "jump" or "run." If your child hasn't said any of these four words yet. Still, you want him talking soon; it may be difficult since toddlers typically wait until they get older before they start speaking in complete sentences. You can still, however, help your toddler learn how to talk. Please start with the most common words; hopefully, he will start putting these words together in sentences in no time!

You can show him what you want him to say, for example, "Milk please" or "juice", but try not to have too much conversation around the word. Try not to keep saying it over and over again. Don't ask him if he wants milk; try saying, "I have some milk" instead. Saying, "Do you want some milk?" is a big no for toddlers. This might create frustration. Also, try not to teach him more than one word at a time. After he says "juice," he goes on to another word but never goes back to the first one until he learns that. The parents should make it fun by demonstrating what we want them to say, showing them how we want them to say it, and giving positive reinforcement when they do it correctly.

Toddlers might use more than the four most common words, and I suggest using at least three to start with. If he doesn't use milk or juice, give him other words that are easy for him. For example, you can show him what sounds like a bottle or cup and get his attention on how long it takes him to say it. Don't force your child to say any of these words; if he doesn't try to say them, don't make a big deal. He probably only needs a few weeks before he starts using some new words, and by then, you'll have noticed that he's starting to talk in other ways.

Some toddlers might prefer to say a few words we teach them, but the majority will still say random words that they think fit the situation. If this is the case with your child, don't discourage him from saying nonsense words. It is suitable for us to hear our toddler's voice and use this to give him positive attention and feedback.

If he has been doing great with these three words, it might be a good idea to go on to more complex sentences. You can slowly introduce sentences after three words. For example, "I want juice, please", "You have juice", etc. You can also do single-word sentences such as, "I want milk", "Is it juice?" or "Where is the cup?" These are all essential steps for toddlers to learn how to talk. Parents mustn't memorize or repeat any of these sentences because, in the process of learning these, our child will experience frustration and a lack of understanding when they don't make sense.

You can also try showing your child your favorite book. (A book can also be your child's favorite toy, a favorite stuffed animal, and so on) Expose him to books that you know he will like. Books that he wants to hear. For example, you can tell him stories about cars or favorite cartoon characters. You can even read nursery rhymes or books with pictures of things he wants to try in the future, like food items or kitchen utensils. It is vital for toddlers not to be frustrated by the book. It should be something that he is interested in. If he doesn't want to turn the pages, it might be because he doesn't care about the book or it's too difficult for him to understand the story. You might want to find a more straightforward book for him with good pictures. In our case, my son picked up any book his hands could reach, held them against his chest, and walked around with it.

If you're teaching your toddler how to talk and you have tried all of these suggestions, then it is time for you to take action. I have found that working with speech therapists is very helpful when parents are struggling to teach their toddlers how to talk properly (if this is the case with your child). You might feel like you're doing a good job and that your child is delicate by himself. You can always benefit from working with someone outside the family and someone who has more experience than you.

It is essential to continue working on speech and language if your toddler hasn't reached his speech development milestones yet. It's never too late to start! Remember that most parents don't know their child isn't developing appropriately until they meet with a professional or their friends ask them, "When will they talk?" If this sounds familiar, it may be time to take action and get your child some help.

Printed in Great Britain
by Amazon